No More Skeleton Winters

Tainted Windows of the Soul

by

Cynthia Reffner

Disclaimer

The word "pedophile" is a filthy word with many vulgar connotations. Just saying it sounds dirty. For this and many other reasons, I have elected in my writings to use the term "Pedi" in its place. I hope, by doing so, it will take some of the sting out of trying to deal with this touchy subject.

Also, I feel that it is important to let you know as the reader that I have chosen to not include any of the actual violations in this story. I have included what led up to the events and what followed. I want this to be safe for all readers and feel strongly that I do not want to glorify any of these vile acts.

Table of Contents

Introduction

A child should be able to pick a dandelion and blow it without any concern of where the wind takes it. This book was written for that child who did not have the freedom to blow their own dandelion. Whether you have been a victim of incest or sexually abused by a stranger, they both are escorted with grief. In one's life, there is a process to completion that needs to take place for healing to both begin and end. The process begins by first realizing that you are hurting. Secondly, you need to figure out or recognize why you are hurting so badly and resolve what you can do to make it better. Three Rs: realization, recognition, resolve. They are each a process. Through this process, completeness of healing can take place. Some people's journey is longer, as was mine, and miraculously some people's journey can be much shorter.

I wrote this book in order to try and help remove the many blindfolds that plague sexual assault victims as best as I can. This book is not for everyone; I of all people get that, but it is for the broken few who are still hurting and in need of help to remove their blindfold. This is my story, my truth, my pain as I lived it. It is about memories that were so painful that I was forced to repress them in order to exist. Memories that I forgot about for nearly thirty years. While it might seem easier for me to just forget about it and not talk about it, that is not in my nature any longer. I have no doubt in my mind that I have been called by the Lord to speak up, speak out, and *tell* of the great and miraculous ways in which God in His divine and innovative way brought me through the healing necessary to come to a wholeness in my mind. Hopefully, this book can help guide you and give you instruction as to how you, too, can begin your healing process.

So often, people in pain, sexual abuse pain, are not given a recipe nor a remedy for restoration to be completed all the way down within the soul.

My hope and my desire are that this book can be just that for you or someone close to you that you know who is still in bondage to the abuse that was perpetrated onto them. While everyone's walk on the trail is different, the end goal remains the same. Healing for the victim. Emotional healing, spiritual healing, and soulful healing as God leads. I have done my best to discuss as many different areas that God walked me through as I saw fit to elaborate upon and write about in order to assist you with your path to healing. To God be the glory for the things he hath done.

The world's ill advice to the victim is to just keep your mouth shut. Keep the status quo. My God says that "That which was done in darkness will be brought to light," and therefore, I will let my light shine. I will open my mouth and speak as I am instructed to do.

Always remember that...*the very moment we pray, the tide of the battle begins to shift.*

It Was Him... Memories Confirmed

Hurry up, is what I thought as I rushed into the house as quickly as my legs could carry me. How many times has the phone rung? My husband, my daughter, my middle son, and I all dashed in from the garage after a night out of eating, each trying our best to reach the phone in our living room before the caller hung up.

"Grab it, Mom... Grab it faster, Mom," my teenage son insisted since I was in the lead. "Hurry up. Get it before it goes to the recorder," he persisted. In hopes that it was one of the three girls he was trying to juggle around in his *dating arena* of a teenage life.

The noise of the phone recorder began to squeal loudly throughout the entire house. No...I quickly reached toward the phone, trying desperately to pick it up before the person on the other end had a chance to hang up.

There was a man's voice on the other end of the line that began talking into the recorder. It was him! I froze inches from the phone. I knew that voice from somewhere. It was the man who had repeatedly molested me for nearly five years of my very young childhood of a life. Why was he calling my house? He was trying frantically to get up enough courage to leave a half-baked apology on my phone's voicemail. My phone? *How dare he*, I thought. Really? You can molest me and ruin my innocence, and is it so invaluable that you think you can just leave an apology on my phone recorder nearly thirty years later? Really? I quickly picked up the handle of the phone anyways. This was going to be good.

I was no longer afraid of him, or at least that is what I told myself. When had I started shaking? Why had I picked up the phone? What was I thinking to not have just let it go to voicemail?

As I anxiously put the phone to my ear, everyone who had just emptied out from the car was standing in the living room and was within earshot of this very volatile conversation. We all froze after our mad dash, surrounding the phone. My family all looked at me, silently sensing that something was up. They all sat scrutinizing his voice and trying to figure out just who the caller was. I, on the other hand, knew exactly whose voice it was on the other end of the line.

It was him! Yep, that was his voice, and it was him. My heart raced. My chest felt constricted. Oh, my heavens, it was him, calling me. Who did *he* exactly think he was calling *my* house? This is my house! My territory! He was not going to intimidate me. He was not going to bully me for one more second of my life. He had bullied me for far too many years. My angry ticked-off heart was pounding out of my chest. *I can do this; I can do this*, I kept silently reassuring myself. He is no longer going to control me. I can have this conversation after all these years because, after all, he is the one on the defense. He finally, for once, was not the one in control. He is the one in the wrong; it just took me thirty years to remember it.

The tides in my mind quickly began to change. He needs something from me. Ohm....why else would he be calling my home and invading my personal space if he were not in *need* of something I owned? My memories. I thought to myself, *Oh, how does it feel to need? How does it feel to have unpredictable moments not knowing what in the world is going to happen next?*

My violator's voice was coming across the lines of my phone. My dark past finally coming to the surface. My repressed memories only being *confirmed* by the one who had caused it all to begin with.

"Hey, Cindy, this is me. Do you know who I am?" he questioned in his eerie voice. Of course, he knew that I knew who he was. He had been my Pedi stepfather for over five years of my life.

"Yes, I know who you are," I responded. My hands were shaking; I could only hope my voice was not. I did not want him to think that he had any emotional leverage over me any longer. He had been my perpetrator for far too many years, and I was not about to give him any power any longer. I deliberately did not speak next; the silence was unnerving. He called me; he can entertain, continuing this con artist of his self-conversation. I looked around at my family, who were staring at me with questions visibly written all over their faces. They were reading my tense body language and sharp tone, which was so much different than the blissful one that was so abruptly cut off with this phone call.

He tentatively continued speaking by saying, "I heard you were going to turn me in to the cops for what I did to you as a kid."

I carefully and methodically responded back by saying, "What would I turn you in to the cops for?" My family's eyes were huge at this point as realization sat in as to whom that voice belonged to that was coming out of the recorder.

"Well, you know..." he responded condescendingly.

"I know? What is it that I know?"

He continued, and I noticed there was a shifting in his tone of voice. He no longer had the arrogant, loud, confident voice he had just displayed only seconds before.

He was on a fishing expedition to see what I had finally, at the age of thirty-six years old, remembered. Bad person. Violator.

He proceeded by saying, "You know I am sorry, don't you?"

I thought to myself, *What is he* not *trying to say?* I answered back and said, "No, I don't. What do you have to be sorry for?"

"Well, you know how I harmed you..." he said, trailing off his sentence.

"How did you harm me?" I questioned.

He said, "Well, you know I touched you inappropriately."

Wow! I thought to myself, *Where is this conversation leading?*

Then I prodded, "And you molested my sister too. Are you willing to admit that too?"

He sarcastically replied, "Yes, I molested both you and your sister. Is that what you want me to say?"

Returning quick-fire, I said, "I want to hear you tell the whole truth. That is what I want to hear you say."

In one of his excuse-filled tirades that were all too familiar to me from my childhood, he responded, "I was really sick back then and didn't even know what I was doing or remember much of what I did to you. I had been drinking most of the time when I would do bad things to you and your sister."

I rapidly returned back in an authoritative kind of voice to him, saying, "So it sounds to me like you are admitting that you molested me, and you are saying you don't even remember most of it. How convenient."

"Like I said, I was really sick back then."

I returned fire in a very aggressive tone and said, "Oh yes, you were really sick, and you tried to impose that sickness upon me."

I wrestled with the fact that I had him on the phone and my family could hear every word he and I were saying. Wow, exactly what I needed my husband to hear. He had sort of questioned the integrity and validity of what I was saying to begin with. So to hear my perpetrator all but admitting this *truth* I had most recently brought to the table, for me, was incredible. Now, on the other hand, for my daughter and son to have to hear it was disgustingly gross. But then again, at least it was coming to the surface and being dealt with. Now, what more did I have to say to this Pedi anyways? I wanted and almost did hang up, but instead, I said, "And you are *not* sick now?" I questioned.

"No, I am not," he stated back at me adamantly.

"Really, and what have you done to change your behavior?" I said. Silence remained on the line. I added sarcastically, "Have you gotten yourself any therapy or counseling? Maybe even gone through any twelve-step programs or a combination of the three?" Still more silence. I proceeded with, "And how do I know you have not molested my baby sister or other family members? How can I be assured you are not still hurting other young girls?"

His response made me sick. He very repulsively said back in a rapid and condescending tone, "I don't hurt the ones that I love."

Oh, he did not just say what I thought he said! Appalled by his response, I was ready to hang up when he quickly spat, "I said I was sorry. I guess that is not good enough. I guess you're going to turn me in to the cops anyways, aren't you?"

I responded with a matter-of-a-fact statement and said, "Well, I'll tell you this much. I certainly will be documenting this conversation and talking to my attorney first thing in the morning. Oh, and by the way, this whole conversation is being recorded as we speak on my phone recorder."

His now timid non-bullying voice responded back, "Well, I have said all I am going to say, and I guess it's not good enough." He tried to back his way out of the conversation he had initiated.

"No, it is not good enough," I said, knowing in my knower he had harmed many young undeveloped girls because that is what Pedis do. They very seldom only harm one victim unless, of course, they are caught right away and sent off to prison. Which, unfortunately, is not the case far too often.

As I frantically decided that this conversation was over with, I hung up the phone, feeling righteous in my indignation. Manipulation. Launch and failure.

Immediately upon hanging up, I rushed to grab a pen and pad of paper to dictate the words that had been exchanged just minutes before as a backup.

My memories were being put into question by many different sources at this point in my life. I wanted my already retained attorney to be on notice that he, the first stepfather, had reached out to contact me, trying to intimidate me into backing off. Insanity.

Within seconds, this elating feeling began to wail up inside me, sort of like emotionally overcome me, and I started yelling throughout the entire house, "I told you, I told you that no good piece of feces did all that inappropriate junk to me." Yes, yes, I yelled, "How does it feel, Mr. Deface (my new nickname for him... so that I did not have to say his name; it made me sick to my stomach at the mere mention of his real name)? Not so good, I will bet. Are you just a little scared now? A little nervous?" As I continued to practically run around my house from room to room, yelling as loud as I could possibly scream, "Hallelujah, hallelujah. He is finally going to be stopped," I hollered out loud! I was a nervous wreck. I was shaking and trembling all over my body. Like a jolt of adrenaline had been injected into me.

Or was he? The fear inside of me questioned myself. Was he finally going to be revealed? Did I sound bold enough? Did I sound unafraid enough? Will he be able to *detect* through the sound of my voice that I truly am still afraid of him, like he did when I was a child?

Then this feeling of fear and a combination of shame began to overpower me, and I started crying and shaking, almost inconsolable. Suddenly, I started laughing and crying at the same time. Crazy. "Finally, finally." I yelled aloud, "He is going to feel just a smidgen of the nastiness that I am living in." Uncertainty of life in general. As my crying escalated, I retreated to my bedroom and began to hysterically ball my eyes out. My body was still shaking and trembling with fear and joy, all mixed up into one uncontrollable ball of confusion. I truly was not sure of exactly how I felt. I had never experienced feelings like this before. Elated that my past Pedi stepfather was finally exposed, and yet I was the one that felt exposed and naked all over again. As if it was all just now happening at that very moment. That is how *repressed memory* works. Awkward.

My husband came into the room and reached out his arms and began to just hold on to me. It was all he could do. I really did not need his educated guess of how I could possibly be feeling; he knew that. He remained quiet and just held me tightly for what seemed like an hour. It was exactly what I needed as a child yet did not receive. Loving husband.

My two children were just walking around in a daze from what they had just overheard. My poor kids, they did not need to be going through what was *my abusive life* and not theirs. They were teenagers. They had their own life experience issues. They did not need more on their plate to swallow. Yet they had been previously filled in on what their mother was going through. I felt they needed to be informed as to what was happening to me. So for this phone call to come across the wires was not a shock to them. They were smart kids, and they could put the pieces together. They realized that the man on the other end of the phone was in *complete denial and repair mode* of his uncontrollable sickness of harming young children.

All these years, I had not remembered what the stepfather had done to me. How can that be? But that is how it was. God had to have allowed me to forget or, as the professionals put it, *repressed it* for my own mental safety, my mental health. I quite possibly would or could not have handled living in the memories of being sexually abused and emotionally being treated like a piece of trash and having to live in the burn-up scared body of over forty percent third-degree scarring.

Repressed No More

Just months prior to this phone call, I had the experience of having one dream after another as I began remembering what it was that *he* had exactly done to me. Yes, I said one dream at a time. That is how God, in His infinite wisdom, elected to help me to recall my memory. *Recapturing* at its finest.

I was in my mid-thirties, married to the same awesome man. Mr. Blue Eyes, I call him. Along with my three children. Three wild-child teenagers. I was working full-time as a licensed real estate agent for what would be my seventh year in San Diego County, California. I had obtained the title of Top Listing and Top Selling agent in an office of over seventy-plus agents. Quite the task. Busy, busy, busy. My husband and I had worked very hard to achieve and achieve some more. That is just how life is in a fast-paced California sales world.

My world was slowly crashing down upon me. I was having a hard time functioning and operating for the past year of my extremely busy high-end job. My emotions seemed to be getting out of control or quite possibly getting in control.

For the past few months, I had been having dreams and waking up with the clarity of these dreams on my mind. As a born-again Christian, I began asking God why I was dreaming about such pathetic things throughout the night.

That is how it all started. That is all it takes sometimes, to just *ask* God to explain why in order for God to go forward in what it is He has already begun in you (Philippians 1:6).

Each time I woke up with another one of these *so-called dreams* fresh on my mind, I began writing them down in my conveniently located composition tablet I had placed alongside my nightstand after my first pitiful foul dream. Smart woman.

Not completely understanding what in the world was happening to me, I still would sickeningly write it down. Once I would reread the dream the following morning, I then would remember it all happening to me as a child. Like it was freshly done to me. Feeling nauseated to my stomach.

I began questioning God. Why in a million years would I have forgotten about this? Goodness. What in the world am I going to do with these very real, raw, fresh, true, valid memories? How could I have forgotten these very crucial events in my life? Emotionally painful.

I was seeing a licensed counselor on a regular basis at the time. After much inner debate, I decided that I would test the waters and tell him about one of these dreams in my next session.

That did not go so well. He stopped me dead in my tracks, cutting me off mid-sentence. It was as if, if he had listened to me, then he was accountable and might get dragged into a situation he did not want any part in. Shame on him. This counselor did not want to hear about it. He quickly stated that this was out of his *realm of expertise* and that I possibly needed to check into seeing someone else who may understand better what I was going through. Quashed.

Boy, was I offended. I had been seeing this counselor for close to two years, revealing some of the most personal abusive parts of my childhood, and he just wanted to throw me to the wolves. Dismissed.

I began looking into finding another counselor who could quite possibly explain to me what I was experiencing. They seemed to be few and far between.

At this time in the nineties, there was a lot of controversy as to whether repressed memory actually existed or not, or so I quickly found out.

Well, for me, it *did* exist because I was living proof it had happened to me and was happening to me all over again. That was all the proof I needed.

I knew in my knower I needed to get these so-called dreams validated by someone who knew more than I did about this subject matter.

Eventually, I found another licensed psychologist who was willing to hear my now multiple dreams and memories of being sexually molested by this first stepfather of mine.

At this point, I had had six dreams of separate offenses. Six. Six separate dreams, all of which after I had each dream, I literally had to ask myself why I was remembering them now. Why now? How could I have forgotten such horrific offenses? It was weird. It was as if after each dream, I would remember it as if it were happening or just had happened to me. I needed to understand more than anything exactly what was going on and how I was going to emotionally survive. I felt like an emotional mess. I needed God's *grace* more than ever.

"The mind is very complicated," I quickly learned from my new psychologist. She called it PTSD. PTSD? I had never really understood it when I heard about military veterans coming home from war with this side effect, but that is how it was being explained to me. "Post-traumatic stress syndrome is exactly what you are suffering from," my new doctor said. Wow.

What was I going to do for employment from here on out? I could barely show up to work without feeling like everyone around me could quite possibly see and feel what a mess I was becoming. I would try and convince myself that they could not see what was going on in the inside of me. For the first time in my life, having everything all perfectly placed, perfectly put on, perfectly taken off was not working. It seemed like no matter how perfect my hair was done or how perfectly excellent I had my brand-named eyeliner on, they all could still see how undone I was in every area of my life.

My real estate career was booming, and I just could not understand how it was that God elected to bring these memories to the forefront of my mind now. "But God is good, and He does things His way, not ours," is what I convinced myself the Word of God speaks.

In addition to working, raising a family, being a wife, and having any type of a life, I was trying to understand how I was going to function with all this emotional pain I was in. What was I supposed to do with all these memories, or should I say repressed memories, I was having?

I needed to be able to keep working. Yet, as each day would slowly creep on by, I was having less and less of an ambition to get to work, go to work, and most definitely, stay at work and perform up to snuff for my very important clientele base. I was losing my drive to succeed. Success was getting moved down on the Richter scale a few notches. At this point, I was having a very difficult time even driving a car without having a very nervous feeling coming upon me. A very important part to being and remaining a realtor.

Not too long after what I knew at the time to be my *fully remembered memories,* I decided I needed to do something to try and stop this old stepfather of mine, should he still be touching young girls. I just was not sure of *the what* I needed to do. I was becoming angrier by the day. Each day that would go by as I was trying to manage my emotions and seemingly failing at it, I was becoming ever increasingly angry. Angry that I was losing my career, angry that my *joy* seemed to be leaking slowly out of me and negatively affecting my marriage as I knew it, and angry basically at the Pedi for the fact that he thought he had *gotten away* with it all. I felt I had to do my part in stopping him from harming anyone else, yet I was angry that it was something *I had to take time out* of my very busy life to deal with.

I knew it was serious because my original counselor basically stated he wanted to *stop* therapy with me. Immediately. As if he were afraid I might say something on the record I should not. I was not sure of all the implications as to why he no longer wanted to see me, but I was sure this new counselor did want to see me, and she was not *afraid* to hear what I had to tell her. I, on the other hand, did not want to hear what she needed to tell me.

You see, after much intake paperwork being completed, turned in, and diagnosed by her, she came up with what she thought was a viable solution. Antidepressants. She explained that I was suffering, along with anxiety, a medium-grade depression. She explained that once I began *dealing* with all these memories, she was certain that this medication was going to help me travel through the pain much more easily. She seemed to explain it all so eloquently. Walking through it all, however, did not seem to feel like it was going to be quite so eloquent.

I was hesitant to graciously and first handily accept her diagnoses. "I can be extremely stubborn at times," is what I told her. "I am a born-again Christian, and I don't feel I need to use medication to *cope* with this emotional pain."

As she was talking, all I could think about was that I did not want to become one of *those people* that I remembered seeing in the mental health clinic where my second stepfather worked when I was a teenager. Those doped up zombie-looking inpatients who walked around with their coffee cup in one hand and a cigarette in the other. No, thank you. Not for me.

As she listened intently to my concerns, she wrote the prescription anyways and told me to "Think about it or, in your case, *pray about it* and at least give it a shot." What did that mean anyways, to at least give it a shot? Is this a hit-or-miss thing? Well, I guess I was about to find out. No one session, quick fix for this gal?

On what would be an extremely long drive home with all those deep thoughts on my mind, I prayed and asked God for His direction and path for me. I asked for Him to open my ears so that I could and would at least listen for His direction, even if it meant using these so-called antidepressants that I was adamantly against.

This is going to take a few searches on the internet, I thought to myself when I got home. Even when a doctor prescribed me a simple antibiotic, I would do all my research and give the poor pharmacist the third degree, and now we are talking about a daily medication that can alter your mind...I'm not so sure.

My next concern was, what would people think of me? I had not heard much about antidepressants at this point in my life, and what I had heard in the local talk shows was not looking so good. I had the impression that they were like a downer, and they scared me. I had overheard a few teammates on my softball league one afternoon having a controversial conversation about antidepressants. A sport I once was enthused with but was slowly losing interest in.

My public persona was already beginning to shift and change with this new chapter, or should I say old chapter in my life. I was barely holding on. If I added these new antidepressants, what were people going to think of me then? Sadly, at this time, I was very concerned with what people would think of me as I made my career in the sales industry. Competitive edge wasting away.

My main concern, even with my limited information guide, was what my Mr. Blue Eyes would think of me. Would he now also think I was crazy, as my mother often accused me of as a child? I had always been very mentally strong. Taking antidepressants seemed to say to me that I was weak, that I was giving *in to* the pain. Would my husband think I was weak? Would he not want to be with me any longer? Was I *damaged goods* now that he knew I was a child of incest as well as a molestation victim? Help me, Lord.

Since becoming a Christian in 1980, I had always gone to God with any of my main issues or problems, and it appeared there were a lot of them rearing their ugly head in my very dysfunctional story of a life. Many of which it appeared I still needed to take to Him.

As I drove home that late afternoon contemplating talking to my husband, I was very leery of telling him about this new prescription that my new therapist had prescribed to me.

Do I tell him what the therapist is recommending? Or do I just ignore what the therapist is saying I need and just throw the prescription away? Do I take the risk of involving his opinion and concern? After all, he does live with me and, for the most part, sees right through me. We were deeply in love after many years of marriage, and with all these *repressed memories surfacing,* I was certain he would have a strong opinion. I just did not know *what* that opinion might be. Concerned.

Or even deeper, I remember at the young age of five or six, soon after I arrived home from the hospital from my long stay as a result of being severely burned (you can read more on this in my first book, *Hollow Family Tree*), I would try and soothe myself from the pain by rocking incessantly on the edge of the couch. I would overhear my mom telling other people that she thought I was crazy. Would my husband think I was crazy too?

What I did know for sure was that I owed him honesty. I made a pact to myself that if he asked, I would tell him the truth. I knew he would ask. Of course, he would ask. He knew most of what I was going through. Or some of what I was going through anyhow; since remembering and documenting my memories, I had begun hiding from him all that I was going through. It was not anything I deliberately did; it was just that he seemed to only be able to *handle* so much, *hearing-wise,* of these sexual abuse memories and of what it was I had remembered. So I only gave him portions of the dreams because he could not handle it, or so I surmised by the looks and body gestures that he would exhibit while I would be talking. Silent innuendos. It seemed to me to almost annoy him each time I would have a memory. I felt compelled to tell him, and yet I could tell it deeply bothered him to listen. He struggled to physically stay present. I can imagine it is like what happens in a relationship when a woman is raped. I internalized his actions and reactions as if I were to blame. He saw with each dream and memory that I was losing more and more of a grip on my ability to function in our busy lifestyle.

There were days when I could barely muster up enough energy to get into the shower. Days when my daughter would encourage me to get up and get going and even persuade me that if I got showered up that she would even blow-dry my hair for me. I never wanted my husband to see that these newfound memories of mine were really dragging me down.

While I am sure he was much more aware of it all than what I was giving him credit for, I still felt shamed by it and wanted to try and not just hide it from him, but to hide it from anyone who I thought might judge me the way *I was judging myself.*

While looking from the outside in, one would think I had a pocket stuffed full of friends, but the truth is I never really allowed anyone very close to me at all. The friend thing was just that, a social thing, nothing close-knit. Just a few close friends and my immediate family, two sons and a daughter and a loving husband seemed to be enough for me.

You see, I always had my life all organized. Or should I say it always *seemed like* I had it all together? House spotless, dishes always neatly placed in the exact right spot in the cupboards, every room perfectly vacuumed, and yard precisely manicured. My hair gorgeously blown out and, of course, the perfectly aligned make-up. My outward appearance had been my shield for my entire life. By looking good on the outside, I thought it did not matter how screwed up things were on the inside. Charade.

Popcorn Ceilings

Each time that I was molested as a child when it was in my house, I would find myself looking up to the popcorn ceilings, as was common in most houses in the sixties and early seventies. I would find myself drifting off in my mind trying to escape the emotional pain of what was done to me. I got good at making faces and objects out of the popcorn surface. I had figured out that I could just stare and stare, going into an almost trance-like wave of the familiar detachment that I experienced when pumped full of morphine not long before when I was severely burned at the young age of four and a half.

Kids are resilient. They will find a way to bounce back. I learned to entertain my mind while my body was being harmed. If it was not the popcorn ceilings, then it was a light socket. I would stare at the light sockets as a point of rescue almost. This sounds so unlikely, orchestrated childhood events, but it is what I did to survive because, unlike some sexual predators, my Pedi was trying to make a connection with me emotionally during his violations, and I could not let that happen. It was my way of putting a wall up to him emotionally and blocking him out. While all Pedis are sick in their mind, my perpetrator was looking for someone to love him back, and it was not going to be me. While I knew that I desperately needed to be loved, it was not going to be from him.

Years later, unbeknownst to me and what had happened in my young early childhood days, I began looking up into the ceilings again and questioning where I came up with the idea and remembered that I used to do that as a child. Strangely enough, it brought me some sort of solace and calm. God wanted to replace this false calm with His *pure calm*, one that only His Holy Spirit could produce. No more popcorn ceilings for me.

Standing Up to Pedi

Make no mistake, the decisions and choices that you make to stand up against your violator or sexual predator will not be easy decisions to make. I am in no way underestimating the guise of the devil in doing so. For me, it was extremely scary to speak up in public. It was embarrassing as a mature adult for anyone to know what I was going through. In the town that I was living in, I was very well known and active in my community, and for lack of better words, I was quite popular (with all my pretentious friends) and well-liked.

In my situation, it was going to take a laying down of pride in speaking out. If I could make any suggestion at all, now twenty-plus years later, it would be to get your support system in place first and foremost before taking on the spiritual warfare facet of sexual abuse. Find a trusted friend. This will take humility, and at this point in your life, humility is a hard thing to drum up, as is trust. You must step out in faith. Ask for their commitment from start to finish while you are walking down this rough and pitted road. If you are married, talk to your spouse. Inform those around you that you trust that you are about to speak out. Ask for their support also. One of the biggest emotional pains that I went through was thinking that I had the emotional support of my family of origin, only to discover that they had mocked me, made fun of me, and stabbed me in the back. One played a private eye type role compounding my torment and mistrust. I would not wish this on anyone. You are already hurting as well as having all these spiritual dark darts shot at you, so the last thing that you need is your family turning their back on you. Sadly, this is the case in more situations than one would think.

Speaking out can be quite frightful. And very eventful. If you think you had drama as a young victim, I am here to tell you that when you begin to spread the word of the sexual offenses done against you, then you have a true drama from start to finish. The reason for this is that you are battling with spiritual warfare that goes all the way back to Adam and Eve's days. There is something extremely deep, dark, and secretive about sexual sin that is perpetrated upon a victim. It wants to snuff you out and shut you up permanently. I am not trying to insight fear or even give fear any power whatsoever, for it states very clearly that "*[My] God hath not given me the spirit of fear but of power and love and of a sound mind*" (2 Timothy 1:7). What I am trying to tell you is to gird yourself up in the full armor of God and don't believe it when others try and tell you that you are only trying to incite a pity party. While in fact, that is the *opposite* of what you are doing.

It has been my experience in understanding the devil and acknowledging his forces of darkness that Satan always accuses you falsely. He tries to make you believe that God never protected you. Well, look who is laughing now because in the pain, through the speaking out, God is using you to help to protect other future possible victims.

My goal in writing this book is for you to get the courage to speak up, but my hope even more than that is that you can speak out and help educate young children so that they can see the warning signs that something doesn't feel right. That you will allow others to learn from your experiences. That they can rise up before they are harmed and speak up and speak out, telling a friend or a parent. And that these friends and parents will start listening to these little ones and their God-given capacity to discern evil. May the generational strongholds be broken for future generations!

It is my firm belief that many people reading this book are at a pivotal point in their life. They are trying to decide if they should speak up, when they should speak up, and how they should speak up. Such decisiveness goes on. For this, I say, seek the face of the Lord. Should you not know the Lord, stop what you are reading right now and open a Bible to the book of John chapter 3 verse 3. Jesus answered the Pharisee Nicodemus and explained to him that except a man be born again, he could not see the kingdom of God. If you do not understand what John 3:3 is proposing, go ahead and read the entire chapter, and it will self-explain about being born again. The reason that this is imperative is that in the standing up to your offender, there are spiritual battles that can and will take place. Having God on your side is one hundred percent an asset. There is territory that Satan has claimed since these offenses were perpetrated against you. Territory that he is not going to easily relinquish. Do not try and fight this battle alone any longer. You have a protector and a provider that has a whole arsenal that is just waiting to go to battle *for* you.

I was a *strong, deeply rooted lover of Jesus,* and yet I was scared to death to stand up against my violator. A supernatural fear. That was how deep the stronghold was. It was paralyzing. Even though I would know that this was what I was supposed to do, and I was putting one foot in front of the other, it was often with a blind faith as each step was taken. I just wanted my life back, and it seemed like every time that I whined and cried to God about how much of my Cinderella life I was losing, it never stopped the mere fact that this compelling, overwhelming *I have to do this* command never lessened. It forced me—yes, I said forced me—to lean into the love of God. God's love was something that I had always questioned being real to me or not. The only thing that could protect me from the fear overtaking me was the love of God. It took me coming to a point of desperation and finally believing what the Bible says that *God is love.* That *God was love.* That *God perpetuates love.* That He is the beginning and the end to love. He would draw me to the Word of God and cause scriptures to stand out to me, and it was in the seeking, in the pressure pot of His molding that the protection from the devil and the dark side of fear came. *The fear,* it had to flee, and *love came in* and took its place.

God expected me to step out in faith in the speaking out against my Pedi. In return, He would protect me with the covering of His love.

Jesus was the exposer and not me. He may use me as his vessel in the speaking out, but ultimately, God was the big bad flashlight. He would make it clear to me that He wanted to use me as a vessel in the exposure of this wildfire of a sin. The sin that was perpetrated upon me—yes, I say sin—had come to a head. While it needed exposing, it was no longer for my protection because, after all, I had already been violated. It was for the protection of other little girls in hopes that they would not be harmed.

Jesus would speak to me, "Do not be afraid. Tremble no more. Be fearful no more but instead cry." Crying did not come easily, for as a child, I was told to *quit crying,* so now, for God to be telling me *to cry* seemed contrary to what my heart knew to do. Your heart feels. When your feelings are hurt, it hurts right there in your chest. My heart had gotten hard and bitter, unwilling to let anyone *new* get close to me, and even those close to me were slowly being shoved away. My little facade of popularity was slowly coming to an end. I quickly learned that in order to protect my heart from hurting any more than it already was, I was going to have to get suited up in the *full armor of God and march forward going into battle.*

If I could give you an ounce of suggestive help, it would be to *believe in yourself.* Believe in your story. Do not let anyone tell you any differently. Always stay prayed up. Fear is just an illusion. An illusion that you can break forth using faith. Forceful, powerful faith diminishes the darkness that is surrounding you. This is a biblically proven fact. Remember that a victim already feels that they have had so much taken from them, and now, by speaking out, how much more are they going to lose? It may feel like loss for a season, but I am here to tell you that God never takes away without replenishing even greater.

One Thing Leads to Another

You know how in life one thing always, yes, always, leads to another? Well, ironically, with all the family stuff happening in our home, my daughter was having difficulties of her own functioning in her new high school. She was struggling with making any friends or even feeling the significance of engaging in the mundane small talk that all the kids around her at her new high school busied themselves with. After all, was not what her family was going through much more important than any history lesson being boringly required of her? Though she was still pulling her high grades, she was having a hard time of her own in the social atmosphere. The effort that would be required to make new friends at a new school was just more than she could bear. Her own *bad choice social life* had just taken a shockingly similar crash, landing her in an unfamiliar school.

One day while she was outside in the quad at school, amazingly enough, just in the manner in which God operates, she happened to overhear two students talking while she was trying her best to stay under the radar. The one girl was boasting proudly that her mom had just passed *the bar* and was finally an attorney. Her mind started racing, thinking about all that her mom was going through. With all the courage she could muster up, she approached the girl and let her know that her mom was going through a traumatic time and could use a really good attorney and a woman at that.

The girl, so excited on her end to help her mom find a client, told Deana that she would bring her one of her mom's new business cards the next day. This marked the *coincidental* beginning of my step of faith. This encounter led me to the attorney that was willing to listen to my story (my memories and my dreams, if you will) to see if I had a leg to stand on in my endeavor to stop this man from touching any more little girls.

"You are not the police... However, I am an attorney, and I think that you could quite possibly have a *repressed memory* case," was one of the first things that this new female attorney said to me. She explained to me that she would have to get approval from her boss to see if, in fact, they would allow her to take the case. After all, she was a practicing copyright lawyer, not repressed memory. Crazy. She would get back to me in the next week and let me know. Within a couple of days, she contacted me and asked for a follow-up appointment where I would sit down with her and go through a written interview prepared by her of every sexual offense done by the Pedi that I had recently recollected. Nerve-racking.

Boy, was I biting off more than I could emotionally chew? Because each step that I took towards stopping this man brought on an even deeper, sharper level of fear that I had never experienced before. So I guess I was still afraid of him. That feeling of fear in and of itself told me that I needed to proceed. I have always been a risk-taker as well as a fact finder. I needed to find a way to make this happen. He needed to be stopped, and I felt commissioned to stop him. One thing that I had learned in my Christian walk is that *fear never comes from God*. And if God allows the fear to come upon me, He will give me the defenses and the know-how to fight up against it.

The next few days, I pondered through my mind just how detailed these memories had been. Something began to mature in my *inner knower* these days that I was pondering. I began to ask the hard questions to myself, like how did he know at the young age of twenty-four when he first started touching me such details on how to perform such vile acts against little girls? It was as if he had a script that he had practiced many different times before. He knew all too well *how* and *where* to corner me. He was educated in how to *approach me, what* to say, *when* to say it and *how* to say it. It was in those few days of pondering that I realized that I was most likely not his first victim, nor was I to be his last. You could bet your bottom dollar that I was going to get to the bottom of it. I might not have had enough self-esteem to step out and protect myself, but being that primary caretaker that I was, I could step out and protect someone else much easier. This inner knowledge that I believe God was revealing to me gave me the *fire* I needed (that I was so lacking in my broken state) to propel myself onward into action.

Exchange of Goods

In my second meeting with the attorney, she wanted me to sign an agreement for payment for representation. She needed five thousand dollars as a retainer upfront. As we were to proceed, and should my case turn into a civil lawsuit, she would need a much larger retainer fee to pad the account in upwards of five thousand dollars. I did not have that. I was just closing an escrow in real estate, and I could come up with half of that. I thought to myself, *Here we go again.* Like many other adventures in my life, the cart before the horse. Here I was trying to just stand up for righteousness' sake, for something that had been done to me, and I was going to have to pay my hard-earned dwindling money to prepare a defense against this perpetrator. Unfair wages.

When I arrived home that day, my husband was not real thrilled with the entire idea. He even said, "I don't think that I can go through with the stress that this is going to cause us," in what I perceived as his cowardly way of trying to bully me into backing down.

I replied, "Well, then I am going to miss you when you *move out* (my bullying tactics being put into action as well) because I am not going *anywhere,* and I am not stopping for *anyone.* I will find a way to come up with the five thousand because if this is what God has called me to do, and I believe it is, then this is what I will do. I will obey God, and God will provide." I firmly spoke back at him. One quiet night.

Two Dysfunctional Love Birds

Through the pondering, I must explain that both Mr. Blue Eyes and I come from extremely dysfunctional, abusive alcoholic homes. And we both took on the roles of *primary caretakers*. Bullies, control freaks, and oldest sibling syndrome. It was a constant wrestling match between the two of us. They say that opposites attract; well, in this case, we were identical. Identicals who had fallen in love carrying all our unhealthy baggage with us. Some bags were tightly zipped up, but some, on the other hand, had gaping holes with filthy garments stuck dangling out of the zipper.

In these days of pondering, I had a few conversations with my husband. His fear of exposure was high. His fear of a loss of a family of origin was great. It appeared to me that he was more concerned about any lights being shined on his own family of origin secrets than me getting righteous indignation against my Pedi. In a crisis, our natural instinct is to suck inward and protect our own walls from being knocked down by others. I, on the other hand, already had all my walls knocked down to rubble at this point. There was no more protecting me. It was now about protecting all the other innocent young children that the Pedi might encounter in his daily life.

So while it would have been more ideal to have my husband's support, it would feel better now looking back at those moments, but that was not our broken reality. After several restless nights of processing, he realized that I was not backing down from this battle. He had hurt me deeply with his indignant words. This was happening. He did love me; he was concerned, and he did believe in righteous justice; he just saw me broken, and he could not fix it. His tactics were not working to slow me down. His response was to try and stop the downward spiral that had so quickly consumed our family, career, and my ability to think and process rationally. He knew that whatever it took, he had to stay strong if our family was going to survive. Sometimes, sadly, that meant him emotionally detaching so he could continue to go to work...after all, somebody had to pay for us living the fast life in Southern California, and it was quickly becoming clear that it would not be coming from me much longer.

We agreed to disagree. He decided that he would give it his best effort of support, but he may not agree with the way in which I was going to go about doing it.

Anxious Driver

I had to meet with my attorney for the anxiously awaited and yet dreaded follow-up appointment. I drove myself, which was very scary with all of the depression, anxiety, fear, and turmoil that I was experiencing on a minute to minute basis, down into the heart of San Diego; I went up five flights of dark underground parking garage levels in my oversized grandiose truck living up to the Jones' city living truck, which looked like it was going to hit the ceiling as I tried to park in one of the economy-sized parking spaces that were offered. The whole time pondering, among everything else, why my husband could not take the day off work to escort me to the attorney's office, hold my hand, and maybe even encourage me. That was not happening. If anything, he was inwardly hoping these obstacles might deter me into changing my mind. To tell the whole truth, I parked the truck and did not instead just turn around and go home by the grace of God. Even though everything on the inside and outside was shouting at me to turn around and go back where I belonged, back in my corner, I put my feet on auto and trusted God that He knew *what* He was doing even while walking through a storm. Battles raging.

I knew going into this appointment that this was going to be a several-hour meeting. She had told me that she was blocking out her morning for me to recall to her all these horrific experiences in detail. And I mean detail. So I marched up to the elevator in the dark parking garage with every fiber in my flesh fighting against the Holy Spirit that was within me that was telling me each step of the way to *keep going*. I hit that elevator button, and once I hit it, there was no turning back. I was opening a can of worms that could not be resealed.

My attorney had prepared me over the phone, a phone call of which I was being billed for in fifteen-minute increments, that there was an urgency to get this case filed with the district attorney. She quoted some statute of the law of which I was oblivious to that there was a *one-year time* frame from the *point of memory* to *the date of filing* regarding repressed memory in the state of California. In order to file, she needed to know the details of every memory that I had had to corroborate the timing in which all the dreams had surfaced.

This knowledge and urgency were aggressively agitating my already felt anxiety that was acting like it was my friend trying to assist me by injecting dart-sized snippets of worry and fear, telling me that I could not do it, bullying me, challenging me to turn around and get back in my truck and go home. It was evilly euphoric. And embarrassingly familiar. Similar to the feeling that you get directly after being molested.

As I walked into the extravagantly designed reception area and was greeted by the young receptionist, I tried to constrain myself and stay as present as possible. I could not help but notice the beautiful oversized marble waterfall of a wall. Such beauty in all my ugliness. I put a fake smile on my face, took a deep breath, and congratulated myself that I had made it to the lobby. This was going to happen, and this was going to happen today whether I liked the way it made my flesh feel or not. I had prayed my way all the way up to this point in the day, and now I just had to have a seat and wait for it to be my turn. Dwindling patience.

While these are the things that I was actively telling myself, the words that were whispering to me louder in my head were that this receptionist seemed like she was expecting me and knew who I was. What all did she know? The all too familiar shame that I could now recall from both being a burn victim and now actively walking in the memories of sexual violation was trying to overshadow me and suffocate me to get me to shut up.

Out walked my attorney. "Welcome. Good morning" is how she greeted me. Such a *normal* greeting for such an *abnormal* circumstance. One that I will always remember the irony of. As I came off from the marble bench that I was sitting on to return my end of her outstretched handshake, I was as prepared as I could mentally be for what was to come. My deepest shameful secrets were about to be put on paper, publicly filed, and exposed for the world to view.

I followed her into the conference room to the very end of the extra-large grand conference table. She pulled out her legal-sized, yellow memo pads and several backup pens. After she offered me a drink, which I declined, she got up and got me a water bottle anyways, along with a box of tissue. Oh great. She knew that this was going to be long and treacherous. We both sat down facing one another. She looked at me with the kindest and most compassionate eyes, and I knew that it was *God's will* that she was in my life. I looked her in her eyes, and I saw kindness and a true Christ-like manner. A kind eye that is not easily found in today's world. I trusted her. In my first meeting with her, I had divulged to her that I was a born-again Christian. She very shortly and professionally stated back to me that so was she. I knew that this was a God thing, and for that, I was thankful.

She asked me, "Are you ready?"

And I said, "As ready as I will ever be."

"Okay, well, let's get started," she stated as she looked at the clock on the wall because, of course, understandably, none of this is done for free. Nine o'clock, here we go.

She started what would be a three-hour-long journey by wanting the time and the date of my first dream or memory, one might say. In addition to the dream, she wanted to know how old I was, where I was living, and as many details as possible. What were the surroundings? What I was wearing down to the finest minute detail. Could I remember colors and the time of day? When I could not remember dates, she would fine-tune the questions as to the time of year, spring, summer, or fall. In addition, she wanted to know what the weather was like. Was it a weekday or a weekend? And as usual, praise God for my impeccably restored memory, I was able to give her defined answers. Amazing majestic moments of time. God is good.

Memory number one took about a half of an hour with all the specifics. Then we started in on memory number two, and she went through the same formatted questions. She must have been really good at shorthand because she was able to match her writing speed with the quickness of my speech. At this point, she got even more detailed down to the street and city of the house location that this violation happened in. I can only assume that as this went on, she got more and more in her groove.

The one common thread in all these violations that stuck out to me was that my mother was never present for any of these violations. My attorney was trying to determine if my mother was going to be liable or responsible for any part of this. I very clearly stated to her that while my mother was abusive both physically and emotionally to the maximum degree as well as neglectful, she was not present in me being molested by my stepfather.

By the time I got to the third memory of violation, I was beginning to gain confidence in my truth. The fear was starting to lift and be replaced with *an all-knowing power* that righteousness was going to *prevail*. By the time we got to the fourth and fifth violations, the attorney was beginning to tear up. There was not a tear to be shed for me. She was the one grabbing the tissue. Hard-hearted.

At about two hours into this thing, we are rounding the corner to get to the end of this interview with the sixth violation. As I finished the details of the final violation, thinking I was almost through the recalling of these horrible ordeals, she started a whole new avenue of questioning. She wanted me to describe what my Pedi looked like, what he was wearing through each event, what his demeanor and personality were like.

I told her that through each violation, he always was drinking alcohol or had been drinking alcohol.

Each inquiry was prefaced with "If you know..." Through all her questioning, she was able to determine that he was a lone wolf.

I never drank any water that day. I did not get up to go to the powder room until it was all done. I was determined to not have to use a tissue for any tears, though I did use one to blot my perfectly lined mascara. I may have been forced to tell these dirty facts, but I could control what I looked like on the outside. I just wanted to get through it. With her probing questions on the specifics on where my mom was and when my mom left and came back, I began to equate and assure myself at the same time as my attorney that my mom was not a part of me being molested. And to my mother's credit, I will give her that much.

Once we got done with the last bit of her questioning, she cleared her throat and proceeded to say the word I could only dream of hearing, which sounded like victory to my ears. She said, "Based on all of the information that you have given me, I think we stand a good chance of being able to file a *repressed memory civil suit* against this *man.*" She explained to me that the next step was for her to get this all typed up in a legal format under the guise of John Doe and submit it to the Los Angeles County Superior Court for review. She explained that it could take at least a month or longer to hear back from the courts.

In addition, she wanted to know if I had a way of reaching my older sister so that she could interview her next. She explained that since this case was treading in *uncharted territory* and that repressed memory cases did not have a good reputation with the court, i.e., witnesses cop out or are no shows when you get to trial. She was already thinking ahead of the game by trying to get her witnesses in line, and she wanted to start with my older sister since we had a shared violation by him. While this had originally started out in what I thought to be a criminal case, my attorney was leaning more in the civil fashion in order to receive a winnable case.

Wow. What an emotional four hours that I do not ever want to have to retread. It was scary. I got intermediate chills, off-and-on sweats. I felt very intimidated and ashamed of the childhood I had lived. And to top it off, I was adjusting to the antidepressants in my system (you get nauseated, spouts of on and off feelings of diarrhea, and really tired). Coffee 101.

Did I really want to do this? Just the memories were hard enough, and now to go through a lawsuit would likely compound all this trauma. At this point, my lawyer had collected my retainer, taken my statement, and oh...let's not forget I needed to try and locate my sister, who last I heard was living on the streets and making her living as a prostitute. Was she still in San Francisco? And my attorney needed to talk to her. How in the world was that ever going to happen? I needed God to help guide me, to direct me, and console me. I needed God to be my *main line* and to get Him off the *side line* where I had so neatly tucked him away and allow Him access into *all areas of my life*.

She finished up the interview by getting as many family members' names, addresses, and phone numbers as I could give her. In addition, she needed the names and addresses of all doctors I had seen as far back as I was able to remember. She asked for my approval and had me sign some different release forms so that she could legally reach out to each one of them and interview as many as possible.

When I left that day and got back into that truck, my adrenaline started pumping. Getting the heck out of this parking garage in one piece did not seem near as difficult compared to this new adrenaline that was running through my veins. My attorney's *validation* and *support* fueled me for my drive home. While the retelling of my memories was horrific, it was just what my attorney needed to hear and know to reassure her confidence and to know that *we* had enough to finally pursue this violator. My job was to wait patiently for our response back from the court. I left that office trying to figure out how I could find my sister; she was the ace in my hole to corroborate these violations. AWOL.

Nervous Courage

I arrived home with a mixture of courage and nervous energy. My husband and kids were eagerly anticipating the details of my meeting. At this point, I had sat down and pretty much explained everything to my three children. I walked into the house being filled to overflow with excitement and victoriousness. My husband, on the other hand, was continually interrupting my victory speech with his concerns about loss of income, my inability to follow through with work appointments, and our inability to stay up to date with our current bills. In addition to the retainer fee, we would have to replenish each month as the attorney bills came in the door. Without me working, which was quickly becoming a problem, he was not so sure that we would be able to afford this civil case. He was not certain that emotionally our marriage could withstand the pressure. But he knew that my integrity and my plight for righteous indignation were not going to stop me. Yes, I had entered into a civil case in hopes of a criminal case to follow. Opposite of how I had first been told it would possibly play out.

I told him that if I had to live in a tent on a campground, now that I knew the truth of what this man did to me, I wasn't going to stop. It appeared to me that he was more concerned about this going public and embarrassing him and about family of origin dissention, and I was genuinely offended. I took that offense and used it as *fuel for my fire* and decided *that day*, "Move over; this is what I am called to do." This Pedi must be stopped.

Through all the muck, I knew deep down that I had what it took to fight this battle to the end because of my previous fight for custody of my two boys. I had already fought one very wicked court battle, which God had allowed in preparation, possibly unbeknownst to me, for what was to come. I knew what it took to stand up and speak my truth now that I remembered my truth, even in the midst of the storm when all might seem hopeless. I knew my God. I knew what He had done for me and what He would do yet again. God sees everything. He even sees when your enemies *take* from you. Righteousness would prevail.

Dysfunctional Relocation

Unbeknownst to me, my younger real blooded brother and my real dad got wind of the importance of my older sister Kathy's testimony and its necessity. Somehow my dad and my brother came up with this idea to go up to San Francisco, where it was rumored that she had been wandering the streets prostituting for drugs. They wandered the streets asking if anybody had seen her and were able to finally track her down at some fleabag hotel. Their goal was to convince her to come back with them to the San Diego area. After three long days of trying to negotiate, they finally were able to convince her to come with them so that my attorney could at least interview her. They explained to her the urgency of how I needed her to be a witness and to corroborate the torment that was our childhood. She agreed to relocate.

I continued to take the antidepressants that I was prescribed, and it seemed to be giving me just enough energy to ignite the confidence that gave me strength and faith to believe that this man could be stopped. While my attorney kept reinforcing the fact that I was not the *child molestation police,* it did not seem to stop me nor detour me from trying to get into contact with little girls (now adults) that I could remember from my childhood that I thought he quite possibly could have harmed. With my daughter and I joining our thought process, we came up with the idea of contacting the phone company and ordering an old-time white page's phone book for Los Angeles County. The place where the offenses took place. And so began the journey... While my attorney was beginning to work this case, I was on a different track. I was looking for witnesses. I had this common-sense feeling that two and two equaled four. That there was no way with the manipulation and knowledge that this man had as a Pedi at such a young age that he had *not* harmed any other little girls. He knew far too much about what he was doing and why he was doing it!

I guess those antidepressants were working. Watch out, Houston!

My ability to work was slowly winding down to even worse than before. Through the years, I had had jobs on and off. Mostly off. And now it was becoming quite the task to perform in the highly amped real estate industry, one that I was quickly losing momentum and interest with. The amount of mental energy that I needed to work was now diverted to this case. When I would attempt to focus on real estate or to gain any new business, I could not seem to stay focused on any one task for a long period of time. Inadvertently, I would find myself thinking about how I needed to be using this precious time pursuing this man who was quite possibly actively harming yet another little girl. I felt an urgency now that I had this knowledge to stop him. I felt like it was my motherly role to protect these innocent children, whoever they might be. I would not turn a blind eye any longer. I would stand firm and fight for even one girl being saved at the hands of this Pedi. The problem was that pursuing this case cost me money, and not working lost me money. Urgency 101.

At this time in my career, there were a few key incidences that helped perpetuate me to not feeling safe while trying to work in an office setting. To put it lightly, the real estate industry, for the most part, is male-driven. To be a woman in the industry back in the '90s was extremely difficult. Especially when a woman is more successful than the man. In my case, they would, in turn, sexually harass me on more than one occasion.

I had been good at *tuning it out* for the most part. Once I began swimming through all these repressed memories, it became increasingly more difficult to ignore even the slightest hints of any sort of harassment. This was becoming more and more difficult to deal with each time I would enter my office.

Mostly, I am sure because of all that I was swimming through in my personal life. It is something that should not take place to begin with, yet it happens every day.

Hello, It's Me

One morning I woke up to a knock on my door, and there was my sister Kathy whom I had not seen for several years.

She said, "I have come to help." She looked unkept and strung out, skinny, and yet genuine in her brokenness. She said, "Can we talk?" She urged me to come out onto the front porch of my house. It was like she did not want to come into my house for fear of being trapped. We sat out on the cobblestone walkway that sunny day.

She wasted no time at getting right to the point. Direct and straight shooters both of us were. She stated, "I didn't know that you didn't remember what he did to us. Did you forget about it?"

She began crying and said, "I was your big sister, and I was supposed to protect you."

"We were little kids," I stated. "How were you supposed to protect me?" We were only eighteen months apart.

"I don't know, but somehow, I have always carried this guilt that you were my baby sister, and I should have protected you," she confessed. I could relate to this because I took that role with my baby sister, who was the Pedi's only real daughter. A child's mind, when not supported by a healthy adult, can rationalize and then carry that irrational thought into their adult life.

I questioned, "So you knew that he molested me?"

She responded, "Yeah, I was in the room one time."

"How come we never talked about it?" I asked. With the realization that the Pedi had threatened us both not to talk about it, we both started to cry. She proceeded to tell me the story of how my younger brother and my dad had come and got her from the slums of San Francisco and how she was now living in the area. She was here to help in any way that she could. She did not make herself into anything she was not. She did not have stability or a life plan but what she did have was *the truth*. The memories that I needed to be confirmed had tormented her for her entire life, propelling her into a life of misery and self-destruction that she existed in.

I contacted my attorney that afternoon and very elatedly let her know that my sister was living in the same city now. Would that help?

Up to this point, one of the problems that my attorney foresaw was that I was lacking a witness to validate that this man was a child molester. My attorney had explained to me that it was her job to inform me that these were very serious allegations and that I had better locate some witnesses to back up my story. She stated that without witnesses, you are walking a very fine line of being countersued for defamation of character. These allegations could ruin someone's life if they were not true. I assured her that these allegations were very much the *truth*. That in and of itself added to the fear that I was already struggling against. My attorney explained that we needed to tread this water very lightly and that we needed to deal with this one *proper step at a time.*

Repressed memory was a taboo subject, one that was hardly mentioned in this day and age, and when it was broached, it was in a *mocking fashion of hocus pocus people* who had been brainwashed. It was something that was not accepted in polite social circles. And even in impolite circles.

Having my sister validate my claims gave me the courage that I needed to walk these steps. I was shocked that she cared and valued me enough to transplant herself in all her own struggle down around our dysfunctional family of origin. Up until this point, she had tried her best to disassociate and disconnect from all the repeated thickness of abuse that was our family legacy. Surrogate sisters, after all.

Prior to this Pedi invading our life, my sister and I were as thick as thieves. For the two years prior to the Pedi entering our lives, my sister and

I had woken ourselves up in the mornings and gotten our own selves ready for school. Picked up our fifteen cents each off of the counter for our daily lunches, marched ourselves out of our dysfunctional house, and walked down the busy street for half of a mile to arrive at the school bus five days a week. We were our own built-in nannies. Watching out for one another. Quizzing one another. *Did you make your bed? Did you brush your teeth?* Always looking out for one another from the wrath of our irrational mom.

The Pedi caused a great divide between us as sisters with his arrival. One that was going to need repairing.

That day I realized that God was on the throne in this situation and that I needed to respect the process. I am the kind of person that wants things done today. *Now,* please...if possible.

There were a lot of unanswered questions, and she had the answers I so desperately sought. The problem was that if I pressed in too quickly, as volatile as she was, keeping in mind, unbeknownst to me, the crack pipe had become her best friend, she quite possibly could go running off again, maybe for good this time, never to be found. So I suggested that we get together and meet in a few days. We had said enough for today.

My brother swung through the cul-de-sac to pick her up; it was a warm day sitting outside. I honestly did not know if I would ever see her again. Would she disappear again? Had I gotten enough information? Could I have dared ask one more question without emotionally pushing her further back into the corner she had become so comfortable standing in? Had I asked one too many?

Pushing these thoughts aside, I needed to freshen my makeup and plump up my hair, tell myself everything was going to be okay, even if I wasn't sure that it was because dinner needed to be cooked and my husband and teenagers were on their way home. I did have many roles that I was expected to play, along with a few past due bills that were staring me in the face. Life was not going to pause for me.

Her showing up that day was my first real glimpse of hope that this can of worms could be opened all the way and that healing could be had for the both of us. You see, with Pedis, I quickly learned from going to the public library with my daughter and checking out the Surgeon General's Report on pedophilia that any time that there are siblings involved, the sick Pedi is most certain to bring division between those siblings, and that is exactly what had happened. In a very curious move on my part, I wanted to understand what motivates a person to harm another child in such a devastating way that they forget about the acts that were done to them in order to survive.

You see, I have a younger sister who was conceived by the Pedi and my mom. My relationship with this baby sister was in strong jeopardy of being lost forever ever since my memories returned. I had concluded, through much thought and prayer, that this was a risk that painfully, I was willing to take in order to reveal what had happened to me. I lost that relationship that year. As hard as we tried (we are, meaning my baby sister and me) to act as if the relationship had *not* been affected that year, the beginning to an end came quicker than I would have thought. But I still had to go forth and speak my truth even at the sad loss of a sisterhood.

Righteousness will prevail. Do not touch little girls on my watch.

Metallic Purple Spandex

Kathy was trying her hardest to be there for me. She was a certified chef and would try to work on and off. Mostly off. Her pain was so deep that, within no time, functioning for any stretch of time present and unassisted from any mind-altering substance was extremely painful. Though she stayed in the San Diego area, she ended up running on the streets of downtown San Diego, very similar to her stomping grounds in San Francisco.

Communicating with her became a very trying task. After several unsuccessful attempts of getting her enrolled into numerous sober living programs, which she always left unsuccessfully uncompleted, she inevitably wound her back up on the streets. They were slowly becoming her blood brothers where she felt safest.

Any time I would try to pick her up on the street corners, she would negotiate, stating that she would only go with me as long as I would promise to return her to a certain street corner at a certain time. She was always fearful that I would trick her and not let her go back. Reluctantly I would comply with her demands.

Not many attorneys had the heart and soul of my attorney. She would make appointments with the promises to keep them with Kathy so she could interview her and get her version of what happened all those years ago on record. But Kathy would not show up. When Kathy finally did show up to my attorney's office, my attorney happened to be at home with her sick kid for the day. Her receptionist called her to inform her that Kathy was there at the office. Kathy was irritated that she had taken the time out of her very busy street life to come in and that my attorney dared to not be there. Entitlement quashed.

The receptionist whispered to my attorney over the phone that Kathy was proceeding to jump up and down on the couch cushions in her metallic purple spandex shorts, shouting and demanding to speak to the attorney. They were able to escort her into a conference room and subdue her long enough for my attorney to graciously make it into the office. During the interview with my attorney, Kathy admitted openly that she was high on speed. She stated that, in general, to the best of her recollection, the complaint that I wanted to file was very close to how she remembered it as a child.

Once my attorney concluded the interview that Kathy punctuated with a slew of graphic and foul language, she let Kathy know that she would get the transcript of their interview typed up and that she would need her to come the following day in order to read and sign the affidavit.

When that time came for Kathy's appointment, she called my attorney's office from one pay phone or another to let her know that she could not possibly come in that day to deal with the whole situation. She proceeded to explain how the initial interview had really sent her on an emotional tailspin. You see, in her heart, she wanted desperately to do what was right and to help her sister, but the pain with the memories of her own that she would have to mull over was too much for her to bear. Wow. Don't I understand that?

Due to the attorney's persistence, Kathy agreed that she would meet Laurie at a predesignated corner in a sketchy neighborhood at a certain time to just sign the papers. My attorney patiently explained to Kathy that she could not just sign them but that she would be required to review and thoroughly read the affidavit in order to assure that everything included was accurate. My attorney graciously met up with Kathy on one of her familiar street corners. Document read. Signature obtained. Downward spiral propelled.

Juggling Act

At the same time, while my attorney was juggling all the interviews with both Kathy and me, she was also simultaneously having read and reviewed my records from doctors that I had been seen by from my childhood in order to validate that I had never *told* anyone about the molestations.

Including in this list was my mother's third husband, who was a psychologist. She was also doing interviews with family members. Because of the repressed memory law, it needed confirming that there was no evidence of my prior knowledge of being molested *ever being exposed*. This whole process was frustrating. Why wasn't my word enough? Slowly, my legal bills were racking up. I had run out of excess money to pay her for all her diligent work.

Meanwhile, my baby sister was calling me, and I felt she was just carefully and cautiously pumping me for information. Well, come to find out, these conversations were inadvertently being leaked to her father, the Pedi. He seemed to be aware of almost every step that I was taking, and his only common source would have been the baby sister. This was her father. She openly admitted to telling him what I, her half-sister who had all but raised her for the first six years of her life, was planning to do. A true conflict. This added even more sorrow to both sides of the table.

I was losing the sister and good friend that I thought I had in the time when I needed her the most. While to my face or over the phone, she would appear as if she were compassionate and had my side, detailed information of all that we were gathering was being compromised. She would have made a good spy, able to infiltrate, gain trust, and abstract all the confidential information. Yet another betrayal in my life. What a mess.

No More Weeds

My marriage was starting to, on one side, get miraculously stronger. The antidepressants seemed to help me get my mood swings under control. My temperament was more balanced. And yet as long as I was inside the walls of my property, where I felt safest, I had a beautiful pool, relaxing Jacuzzi; you know, the white picket fence. But you get me outside of my house in a public arena with my teenagers, and panic, anxiety, and doom would hit me. I felt a responsibility to be a part of my teenager's lives...baseball games, shopping mall, local corner taco shop. All the while edging to get back home where I felt safe and no one would hurt me. Yes, I say hurt me because that is how I constantly felt, the eeriest feeling that I could not seem to shake even through prayer. While I never quit praying and believing, in the shadows was always lurking this horribly dark and dreary fear. It was a double-edged sword. My very well-kept life as I knew it was being exposed as being an untended garden.

In this time, God gave me a vision to not till up the ground but to allow Him to do the tilling. You see, currently, in my life, I was doing a lot of journaling every day in the early morning hours. I figured that since this hidden secret was coming to light, I might as well deal with everything. I might as well deal with all the pain and quit running. To me, it was like planting a garden, getting it all tilled up, and while you are at it, get every little weed out of the soil. Little did I know that in all that journaling would be included the contents that would go into my first book, *Hollow Family Tree*, as well as this book. I figured that I might as well deal with the alcoholism, the emotional abuse, verbal abuse, physical abuse, and the pain from the horrible accident that I endured at four years old, resulting in burns. Get it all out on the table.

Up until this time in my life, I have never been close with my mom, but for a short stint, while all of these memories were surfacing, she was one of the only people that could corroborate the different scenes in these memories that I could ask pointed questions to validate what I was remembering. And of course, every single time, yes, every single time, I would ask her refined details, and she would *adamantly* deny them. Rebuking me with her tone. Almost accusing me of being a liar with her subtle hints made in a questioning fashion. Only to return days later with each event acknowledging certain facts that I had specifically pointed out. Typical. You see, she was in denial herself. She knew that he had molested my sister Kathy. So it only made sense, with all the emotional issues that I had dealt with through the years, that there was a great likelihood that he had molested me also.

Through much travail and multiple phone calls back and forth, she, little by little, came out of denial. She would call me and admit that yes, in fact, something was a certain color; yes, something was a certain way; yes, he did have a pick-up truck for a short time; yes, he did wear a black polo shirt with golden embroidery, and yes, he did borrow a boat one time on a camping trip. All the specifics of each memory, little by little, she began to acknowledge. She, too, was having her own blindfold removed as she began to realize that, yes, he had molested me multiple times.

While having conversations with my mom was not at the top of my list because alcohol was on the top of her list, I would learn quickly to time my phone calls before four on a weekday and definitely not after twelve o'clock noon on a weekend if forced to call. You never knew which Jekyll or which Hyde you were getting in her drunkenness. But I needed her memories. In need again.

While at the same time my mom was having deeply personal conversations with me, she was relaying them to the Pedi's daughter, causing an even bigger division between my baby sister and me. Dysfunction at its finest. *Triangling.* Each validation that my mother would give me regarding my memories and how it really was only gave me fuel to fight for the right to be free emotionally, spiritually, and sexually. After all, those are the three areas that the evil Pedi had me in bondage.

Tainted Windows

My relationship with the Lord currently was raw and exposed wide open for God to till my fields. This was the perfect opportunity for God to plant on good soil. Fertile soil. He had given me a good life loving and devoted husband and three kids that loved the daylights out of me. He had unlocked all the hidden tainted windows of my soul. I felt a freedom to enter into the greater things that I knew that the Lord had for me. *No more skeleton winters for me.* That term is just a term between me, my sister Kathy, and God. You see, I would go through seasons in the spirit realm where I felt like God had put me out into the cold. Where He could not hear me. Where I could not hear him. I could never quite understand it. But God does not come off the throne due to the lack of my knowledge of knowing Him. And He was not going to change anytime soon. I had to make the change.

There had always been a divide, like a gully, if I might say, and I never could understand it. I never could figure it out. But now I understood it. That gully was a representation of my lost memories that God wanted to bring to light. God walks in truth and in light, and in Him, there is no darkness. And so, therefore, He did not want me to be in any darkness any longer. He had to bring my soul into the light and healing, and He did just that as He promised in Isaiah.

"And it shall come to pass, that before they call, I will answer; and while they are yet speaking, I will hear" (Isaiah 65:24).

He brought back my lousy memories, or as the world would say, *repressed memories,* by way of dreams throughout my many restless nights.

Some might say dreams. Yes. That is exactly how God, in His infinite wisdom, chose to speak to me, show me, and reveal this to me. Throughout my life, God has often spoken to me through dreams. God speaks to those who listen and to even some who do not. One thing I know for sure is that when God speaks, it is *to provide for you* or *to protect you* from something even worse than would have happened had He, God, not have stepped into the middle of a situation. He is a wise God.

While I was so busy trying to gain the whole world and all that it had to offer, I was losing my own soul to the darkness. But I am an overcomer. I am called of the Lord. I am a fire starter, pole bearer, and a watchman. I know the Word of God. And I know who Jesus is, was, and is to come. God would not take me through a gate that He did not open. Because in His Word, He says that we are His sheep, and He is the shepherd of the pasture. If He told me to step through it, then I must obey.

While I had pretty much lost my career at this point and was not unable to hang onto any new business, little by little, I had no income. My energies were going toward putting a big fat stop sign up to the Pedi. Not worried about gaining the whole world any longer but in having my soul restored to a point that I could even remember wholeness all the way back through my childhood.

Much to My Surprise

The next thing that I knew, I was getting a confirmation from my lawyer that she didn't think that it was going to be possible to go after the Pedi criminally without more victims or witnesses coming forth, but that just in case, should we need a timestamp down the road, she wanted me to file a report with the sheriff's department in the county that the crime occurred, Los Angeles County. I called my local sheriff's department to see if there was a possibility that they could do a *courtesy report*, and they graciously agreed.

I knew that it was going to be very embarrassing for me to sit down with a complete stranger, quite possibly a male, which I had grown to dislike. I would have to have perfect timing for that. You see, my husband was a shift worker at the time. And my daughter went to school Monday through Friday in another city, so I had to figure it out so that the sheriff could come to my home when my husband was not home, but my daughter was by my side to protect me. As I look back on it, it was quite sad, but it was what it was. Where my husband was lacking in compassion, my daughter was growing to the overflowing.

Having the sheriff come out on a Saturday was the plan. Husband at work. Daughter home from school. Knock at the door. Sheriff came in. The interview lasted approximately two grueling hours. Humiliating.

The officer was in his mid-thirties, and yes, he was a man. He knew what he was coming there for, as they had done a mini interview over the phone prior to setting that standing appointment. I often wondered if they hand-picked the right officer or if I should say God hand-picked the right officer to come to my house that day. That would be just like God to pick a gentle-natured male to show up at my home, in authority, and enter my private zone where I felt the safest.

I welcomed him in as politely as I could, given the situation. For you see, I was at his mercy, and he was doing me a favor. What a dreaded day that must have been to him to listen to the details of what had happened to that poor child...which sadly was me.

The cool thing was that unbeknownst to me and much to my surprise, he took down every word that I spoke as if it was the gospel truth. Something my own family could not even seem to grasp. This stranger gave me the *gift of belief.*

Notepad after notepad, he scribbled at times, tearing up himself. As if it had happened to one of his own family members. I believe this was another one of the foundations of new beginnings for me. A fresh chance. A new opportunity to begin to trust the male species.

While being interviewed, I began to shake and tremble on and off. My truth being exposed on paper to this unknown man amazingly caused what this Pedi had done to me to become even more of a reality. Upon completion of filing an incident report, as they call it, a solemnness came over the officer as well as myself.

It took the power of God for me to file the report that day. Because as much as I wanted to stop the Pedi, I certainly did not want to tell my story to a stranger. But like I said earlier, *no more skeleton winters*. No more running out into the *cold emotionally* and refusing to deal with the pain.

Melted Chocolate Chips

Imagine for a second how it would feel to just be minding your own business on your day off baking your chocolate chip cookies, having to recall the dream that you had just had the night before. Repressed memory with regards to sexual violations just flat out makes you feel vile. I would try to function to any onlookers, kids, husband as if I had not just been exposed. I always knew that my childhood was not functional. I had suffered numerous childhood abuses, and now with these new memories, I was being degraded once again. No longer.

The first offense, childhood molestation, that I remember is when my stepdad entered the room, and it seemed peculiar that he was only wearing underwear. I thought naively to myself, *You need to go put some pajamas on.* I knew that he had been drinking quite a bit that night. He just casually sat down on my bed and began pleading with me about the importance of why I needed to call him daddy. When I did not immediately jump on his sick bandwagon and begin calling him daddy, he started to plead in his desperate attempt to convince me. He began inquiring with question after question. "Don't I provide the food that goes on the table? All the pretty little dresses you wear, don't they come from me? Don't I deserve to be called daddy? ... Please call me daddy... Won't you please call me daddy?"

He was trying to validate his worth. And why he was entitled to be called my daddy. It was almost as if he just came in the room that night wanting me to begin to call him daddy while at the same time he and my mother had decided to change our last name to his last name. It was supposed to be this wonderful charade. In the sixties, it was still very shaming in society to be divorced. He was desperate to cover up the shame and brokenness. I guess he was looking for his white picket fence of a life, which included me carrying his brokenness.

When I did not yield in my response, he molested my sister and me that night. Crazy how a child thinks. I blamed myself. I would tell myself, *Man, if I had just said that it was okay to call him daddy quicker, then maybe he would not have done that to me. He was trying to punish me,* is what I thought because I did not agree immediately as to his advice, his reasoning why I should call him daddy.

You see, Pedis are emotionally weak people. They depend on their victims to carry their pain. Prior to sexually molesting you, they involve you in an emotional incest. This *won't you call me daddy* thing was the beginning of that very sickness being perpetrated onto me. How was I to understand at six years old that he was experienced in this Pedi profession as he began to proceed with me in making our family look whole? Calling him daddy was going to help with appearances.

Here I was the victim of child abuse, and my personality type wanted to figure it all out. Why? Why would somebody do that? What would motivate him to do that? Let us get to the bottom of that. But it served to my benefit at this time in my life.

He would say to me, "Who is going to buy those pretty little shoes that you like so much or those cute little dresses that you wear...?" In my case, in the first two years of my mom's marriage to the Pedi, I had little or no contact to my real dad. So my violator would add, "Your dad surely isn't going to buy them for you. He is nowhere to be found," which was a bold lie.

My dad was just not given access to us children for two years because the Pedi had my mom convinced that we were best off as a family without my real dad involved. He persuaded her that we would be a closer-knit family if she would just cut my dad out of our lives. As a child, you are not given all the adult information as to what is going on in your home. So if you have a hateful parent who had separated you from the other parent, it is really easy for the Pedi to sweep in and mask the truth of the fact that the other parent does love you. This is prime breeding ground for the Pedi. They play on hate and mistrust. My mom and dad's marriage had failed, and my new stepdad played on the hate that they both held toward one another. My dad was given summer vacation court-ordered time of ninety days with us kids in the summer. This did not stop my mom from doing her utmost to keep us from him. He depended on the hate toward my real dad to fuel his sick obsession. He chose a woman who was so broken and fully revengeful from her first failed marriage to manipulate and strategize and con. To take advantage of her distraction and use it to his advantage to fulfill his own sick agenda.

My mom had a habit of keeping the bathroom light on and pulling the door mostly closed. Well, that night, the light went off. Poor man's night light. As he entered the room, I began feeling anxious and fearful. Who knew what he was coming in my room at night for?

That was my first recollection of being violated by the Pedi; though not the first violation, it was the first one that I recalled at the time.

As I stood in the kitchen, a mom and a wife, pondering this vivid memory that came to light the night before, I just needed to make sure that every chocolate chip was in the right place in every cookie. Because I could not change the dream that I just had, but golly, I could make sure that each cookie was perfectly golden brown. Perfection in my unperfected life.

You see that when you are remembering these dreams, trying to live, breathe, respond, and survive, you are still having to live real life. I had always gotten a release through baking; it always gave me a *high* that I could perfect a cookie, yet I could not quite perfect my own life. Especially now. But I could at least try.

I thank God for His Holy Spirit's intuition because He gave me enough common sense to write the dream down. While I did not recollect every specific part of the dream, it was enough to wake up my long-repressed memory. As I would go about my business each day, I could work through that dream and bring it into reality. And majestically, it was as if my brain woke up, and I would remember the actual event just as if it had just happened to my body. Living in it would prove to be quite difficult.

I was seeing my doctor once a week at this point, trying to work through my unexplained anxiety. On my next visit, I told my doctor of this memory that I had had and the specifics. It disgusted me. When you talk about a dream, memory is similar to having a bad stomach flu combined with coming down off the drop from a really high roller coaster on how it makes your stomach feel but also how it makes your mind feel scared. The incident needed to be told and validated, and I knew it. Baking those cookies that day gave me the time I needed to process just a minuscule of the pain that I was feeling, never realizing that it would take me twenty-five years to finally write about it. At first, I thought that *I can get through this. This happened to me. I can process it. God is a healer. God is a deliverer.* I thought that it was just a one-time thing, not realizing that there were many more violations and molestations that God was going to reveal to me through even more dreams.

In the months to come, I would have five more separate molestation, violation dreams and memories. All of which required a trip to the grocery store, butter, butter, and more butter. I baked my way through it, much to my family's delight. Many times, baking multiple items at one time. The more I could juggle, the more perfect I could try and make myself feel. I began to realize how imperfect and broken I felt on the inside. So what better way to try and remedy the problem but to make sure all my cookies were in a row? I bypassed many a meal just to eat a cookie. You see, I had always kept my weight fairly maintained, but something was beginning to happen in me. From the very beginning of the memory of that very first molestation, while it might be hard to understand because I certainly did not understand it, the quiet little child in me was screaming out, saying, "Feed me." This was certainly something I needed to talk to my doctor about.

Polished Words

What always amazed me when I got older as I remembered the sexual violations was how polished he was at knowing just what to say to a six-year-old child. Adept.

It would be those polished words that would torment me in my dreams at thirty-five years old after remembering the sexual violations that occurred. It would be those perfectly worded sentences that would cause me to seek the face of the Lord as to what else had happened to me. It would be those acted out actions toward *me,* the child, which would cause me to go to a more knowledgeable counselor. Yet, it was God's divine Holy Spirit's prompting that gave me the wisdom to tell the counselor, to document the sessions, as well as my first recollection of the Pedi molesting me.

I believe all active Pedis are driven by dark forces. I believe they may start out oppressed and tempted to act out their fantasies, but when they act out on those dark, evil, lustful thoughts, they eventually invite demons to enter their *being,* ultimately becoming demon-possessed.

So, of course, those demons cunningly escorted my Pedi to my bedside to violate my body once again. Keep in mind that my physical body was still recovering from third-degree burns from over forty percent of my body. I was still all bandaged up for the most part. This takes an extra evil person to deliberately harm an already brutalized victim. Foul. Depravity.

My Pedi would say that he was sorry when he was finished violating me and that he would not do it again. Almost in a tearful voice, he would explain how sorry he was. He would always close the violation with *the same old song and dance* about how it would help him out so much if I would just call him daddy. Eventually, of course, I would agree, but I never did call him daddy. There was one daddy that I knew, and he was far away, nowhere to be found.

It was not him. Sicko.

He would leave that night warning me not to tell a single solitary soul, and then he would add, "Who is going to believe you anyways?" I treaded the ground lightly, being such a bother to my mom. Would I dare tell her what was happening to me? After all, the Pedi had done his best to convince me that I was not worth being believed. Many times, he had heard my mom yell at me and call me every name in the book, including worthless. He would walk by shortly afterward and whisper, "Told you so...told you that you were worthless."

What was I to think? Every way I turned, I was in the way. Small house.

I would usually retreat to my bedroom or head on down the street if I could get out of the house to escape and see a friend of mine, anything to get out of the way. You see, inside, I was emotionally dwindling away to nothing. Every thought that I had, I questioned its validity. My value was reducing day by day, second by second.

One day while my mom was in the kitchen cooking dinner, she was getting ready to go bowling, and we knew that she was going to leave us home alone with the Pedi. When my sister protested, they all three went into the bedroom to have a talk privately. My sister confessed that he had done something foul and sexual in front of her. My mom, for whatever reason, possibly to get a cigarette, left the room, leaving Kathy all alone and at the mercy of the Pedi. He instantly switched into a threatening whispering rant, trying to convince Kathy to take it all back and say that she lied. Sadly, he was able to convince Kathy to say that she was lying to my mom. My mom entered back into the room, and Kathy did exactly that.

In my mom's deep denial of drunkenness, she believed my stepfather. Believed he was the one telling the truth. Wow, really? In what world does a young girl make up such horrific imaginary stories? Where would she begin to even know these things to make them up? I was not even going there. I had watched my sister come forth and tell what had been done to her to no avail. Who was I to think that *my speaking up* would be any different? My mom already disliked me on many different levels. I did not need to add to her hate and discontent for me.

In the memory of it all, as a thirty-five-year-old adult, I began to quote scripture back at the Lord.

"Unto thee Lord will I cry, O Lord my rock; be not silent to me: lest, if thou be silent to me, I become like them that go down into the pit" (Psalm 28:1).

As each new day went by, I was finding it more difficult to follow through with just about any task. Follow through, up until that point, was my strong suit. Just ask my teenagers. I would wake up each day and try my best to start out fresh. Forgiving. Not feeling forsaken. Because a part of you having to walk through this pain can kind of make you feel like God had forsaken you. I would go to my favorite chair and read God's Word. Pray and ask God to please get me through this all. Still trying to work, I would proceed to get ready to go out into the market place yet all the while, I would be talking myself into just going back to bed and rolling up in a big ball, lying around thinking and thinking all day long. I was in some really deep pain, trying to figure a way out of it. On the days when I would have to function outside of my home, I would give it my best effort. There were so many times when I felt that God was being silent toward me, and it would cause me to cry out for help.

"Hear the voice of my supplications, when I cry unto thee, when I lift up my hands toward thy holy oracle" (Psalm 28:2).

I would plead with God that I was an upright servant. I was trying my best to make myself get up and be accountable to this world. I would cry out for God to please help me make it through another day.

The Three Cs

My stepfather was a very cunning, charming, and convincing man. He was a hard worker with a follow-through work ethic. He loved the almighty dollar. He was very boisterous and bragged about anything that he accomplished. He loved to be the center of attention in any room that he occupied.

My mom had found him in one of the bars that she frequented. *What could she expect?* I would ask myself as I lay in my bed. Had he chosen my mom because she had three young children? Probably. Was he on the hunt? Had he just recently moved on to new victims? Whom else had he harmed? Had it happened to him? He knew far too much. Pondering. These would be all the questions that would circulate through my mind thirty years later as I began remembering these repeat violations one by one.

Days would run into weeks; weeks would run into months as I would try my best to fulfill my obligations to my clients. You see, in the real estate field, you represent both sellers and buyers. I enjoyed representing sellers the most. The problem was that the *extra work* that it took to represent a seller was far more tasking than driving a buyer around from house to house. Little by little, I reduced my listing base as best I could. My income was quickly beginning to dwindle. I was not coping well at all.

As I awoke one night in a hot, miserable sweat, I began remembering another violation pushed on me by my Pedi stepfather.

I recalled being home sick one day from school. I was about seven and a half years old. I had a double ear infection and was congested and had a sore throat to boot, something that was common with my weakened immune system. While my mother had gone out for a few hours, I decided to use what energy I could muster to try and take my morning bath. I felt lousy. Just as I finished bathing and was getting out of the tub, my stepfather entered the bathroom. He made me do unspeakable things to him. Once he had achieved his goal, he left the bathroom and me behind dismissively, saying, "You know what to do. Go ahead and get cleaned up."

I returned to my lukewarm water that was anxiously waiting to soothe my troubled soul. I sat and cried. He was at it again. When was he going to stop? Sad. *Why can he not just leave me alone?* I thought.

Not long after I reentered the tub, I thought that maybe I would be better off to get out and get dressed quickly before he could change his mind and return to do it again. Fear struck the depths of my soul. Anxiously and in a frenzy, I hurried out of the tub and rapidly got dressed. I rushed into the living room and continued lying on the couch that was planted in front of a low-volume TV, feeling and reacting as if I had done something wrong. Really? *Leave It to Beaver* was on the TV. I remember thinking how I wished I really had a loving mother like the beaver had. At least his mom instinctively knew when beaver had gotten into hot water.

My mom arrived home shortly after I returned to the couch. I remember feeling a seething anger toward her. How could she not witness that something was not right? Did she even care? If she did, you sure could not tell by the way she spoke to me and treated me so unkindly.

I did not tell that day. Again. Who would believe me anyway? How many more times would I need to remember? I was sinking into this quicksand of memories faster than I could get out of the last violation memory.

"Dearly beloved, I beseech you as strangers and pilgrims, abstain from fleshly lusts, which war against the soul" (1 Peter 2:11).

So sinful, lustful thoughts and sinful, lustful actions do, in fact, war against the soul. The Bible says so. Yes, the Bible says it, not me. So to be sinfully and lustfully touched or thought about by a Pedi warps the soul. If a Pedi desires to harm you by sexually touching your body, your soul will need mending, fixing, restoring, and healing and deliverance. It needs to be reinflated with holy healing with what was robbed from the soul to begin with. Peace. Internal innocence. Self-worth. Self-confidence and reasonable knowledge of who you are. Who you were. Who you could have been.

There is a reason that God tells us to stay away from lustful actions. It turns to disaster and destruction. Interestingly enough, one definition of "lustful" is "unusual ungodly desire." Inordinate desire. The definition of "lucre" is defined as "dishonest gain." "Filthy" is defined as "nasty, dirty beyond repair and cleanliness." These are the feelings that I was carrying. This memory would deepen the sadness that I was already suffering in. How could any person in their right mind do such horrific acts to a child? What was wrong with him? My anger was beginning to mount to its highest form to date.

The Good Fight

At times, my faith in God seemed to appear lost, but I continued to keep up the good fight. I kept pressing into reading the Word of God daily, even when I did not feel like doing so. I felt compelled to add the gospel to my life daily. Keep in mind that when these violations originally occurred, my body was still healing from being severely burned. My scars were still sore to the touch. And yet he was so freely touching me wherever he saw fit. Disgusting. These memories were hard to handle. Truly he was an emotionally sick man. Scripturally and spiritually, he was void without an understanding of the lasting impact of what he was putting into motion.

Still trying to continue to work my job, my brokers could see that I was going through something, but they never asked me what it was. I never told them either. How could I? Would they have really cared? They were in the business to make money and not to have concern for why their top female agent's performance could not maintain. I would go through all of the motions day by day, with each day bringing new fears.

God Still Hears Me

"Therefore I will look unto the Lord; I will wait for the God of my salvation: my God will hear me" (Micah 7:7).

I was determined that no matter how dark it got, God could still hear me, even at times when I could not hear Him. I would cry out to God minute by minute, day in and day out. The pain was immense and emotionally intense to carry around with me. No wonder God saw fit to postpone this torment until I was better equipped to handle and process it. I knew enough from my old Bible study days that God would never leave me nor forsake me. No matter how far out there I was in my pain, I knew that God would not leave me stranded. He loved me, and the Bible told me so. I knew that somehow, He was making me more like Him each day; I just could not explain how. His angle of healing came with much resistance from me. Anger toward my Pedi was ever escalating. I thought to myself, *How many more memories will surface?* How many more memories did I really need to go through to be made whole? I knew in my knower that as these memories surfaced, God was somehow making me whole. Such a perfect God. *How could that work?* I thought. I was remembering these vile, foul, and unspeakable sexual violations happening to me as if they were happening to me at that very moment that I would recall them. How could that be healing? Then God would bring this scripture to my heart and mind.

"For nothing is secret, that shall not be made manifest; neither anything hid, that shall not be made known and come abroad" (Luke 8:17).

Could God just take me back to the place where all I did was walk in His presence? All I wanted was to spend my time in praise and worship. Or would I always be in such a desperation mode, coming to God in such daily despair? Oh, how I wanted those voluntary days of praise and worship back again.

This place of being so desperate for God to intervene and help me through all these wicked emotions was beginning to wear on me.

I was still taking my antidepressants faithfully and at the same time each day as prescribed. Each home that I would close escrow on, I would tell myself that it would be my last. However, my family had become accustomed to a dual-income, and I had bills to pay. My teenagers were growing in their wants and needs. College was just around the corner; I had to keep working. "I cannot let my children down" is what I would tell myself to keep going on each day.

When I had entered the industry, I had a lot of friends who were in the need of being homeowners. They kept me rather busy year in and year out. My real estate friend volunteered to help me while at the same time training and educating me about the industry. This seemed to work for the both of us, and we got along well. So a team we became. She was a blessing to me. However, by the time all these memories surfaced, I ended up quitting that real estate office to move to an office closer to my own home. My three teens were starting to act out, as most teenagers do. In moving my office closer to my home, I hoped to physically get home quicker in times of teenage crisis, and there were a few, quite a few.

No Heathens Here

Trying to keep a home intact was startling. It was becoming more and more difficult. While my teenagers had their moments of level-headedness, the pot smoking, cigarette smoking, and binge drinking were becoming more and more the norm for them in their fast-paced high school. I did not raise my three children in the house of the heathen, and no matter what I was going through, it was not acceptable, and nor would I just lie down and let my children walk on me any longer. This was another issue that God was bringing me out of denial about. Rebellious teenagers!

On the other hand of the spectrum, my husband was having to travel for work to the other side of the United States for the electric company that he was employed by. He would be home for two weeks and be gone for three. Panic. This was causing me undue pressure. But he needed his job, so travel it was. When he would be out of town, it would seem that each teen had their own personal agenda. They sat their sails on flying the cope, being disruptive and adamant. Disobedience to the max.

So I had to pull up my bootstraps and get a grip and carry on as if nothing were happening to me. Wow. Could I do this? I had to.

Once my kids were at school for the day, off to work, I would go. I had a computer at home by the early nineties, so working from home became all the easier. Just to get up and go into the computer room was all that I could do some days...but I did it.

Word of Cleansing

Just prior to the memories surfacing, I began struggling with OCD behaviors to the max. I would lock my car doors and then return to the garage to make sure that my car doors were locked two, three, and four times every night. I would lock my bedroom door, get into bed, and within minutes question whether I locked my bedroom door. Over and over, night after night. Truly I did not know what was wrong, but something had gone awry. I asked God, "What is the problem here?" Why was I doing these behaviors?

There were times when out of the blue, I would begin to cry. (As a child, I was taught that it was not okay to cry.) I would immediately try to dry it up and quit crying because *only babies cry*. Was I a baby? No, then I needed to quit crying. Head trip.

In my adult years, God gave me a word of encouragement in my journals. He spoke...

"Let your tears, Cindy, be a form of cleansing. A cleansing of the inner soul. Let Me bring light to your soul. Allow Me to go down into the cave of your soul. And I will light a candle of life. I will hold the candle of life. Be still as I hold the burning candle, and you will know that I am God. The God that healeth thee. Let us spend time down in the cave of your soul. It takes time to heal. We need to be patient and careful. Remember in the Word how I teach you not to tear away the wheat from the thorns? As you sit and allow your soul to be healed, I will not leave you. I will never leave you alone. When you cry, cry to Me. I can hear all things. Do not turn away and cry as if I cannot hear you, just as you did when you were a young child. But rather turn and lift your face to Me, and I will hear your cry, and I will comfort you. As a child, you were not comforted; you were left alone to weep. No longer shall you weep alone. I will give you My shoulder to cry on. Do not take the tears with you. Leave them there on my shoulder. Do not wipe your tears in shame anymore. I will turn your tears into joy. Your mourning must take place for you to be whole. Please do not hide anymore.

"The healing that I want to complete within you and around you will be lengthy. It is not a process that I can perform instantly. If I could, Cindy, I would, just for you. However, your healing will touch many. The process is a will to the completion of the journey in your life. One day soon, you will be whole. You will think back and know that it is better to give healing than to have received healing. Because in giving of your healing, you are giving from health, from wholeness, and receiving healing, you are being restored, and restoration takes time for completion. You are walking exactly where I want you to walk. You are waiting well. Remember the word 'soon.' And hold onto this word soon. Continue to seek Me. I am going to heal your mind. I am going to heal your memories. I am going to heal your thoughts of past pain. Before you know it, you will be one dynamic, healed individual. You are where I want you to be. Hold your head as steady as you can and let Me go forth and do the work. Let Me complete your restoration."

Interpretation of the Word

At that moment in my life, I was having a really difficult time giving up control. This word, while it was encouraging, was also somewhat of a reprimand and word of correction. If you go back and evaluate and reread this word that God spoke to me, you will notice the commanding words within this word. He was telling me to let Him in. Let Him do the work. Let Him use His godly power and be the God that He is. And that in my obedience to obey, there was going to be no partial healing here. If I would obey Him and cry out to Him, then there would be a connection made, reattached if you will, like a severed electrical cord. He would wind each section back together, perfectly pairing it up, enabling Him to turn on the lights within my soul where darkness had once resided.

"And He said unto them, this kind can come forth by nothing, but by prayer and fasting" (Mark 9:29).

So I proceeded forth to the best of my ability and better than I ever had before by remaining present, no longer reaching back to the emotional skeleton winters of my life to try and sustain me. Instead, I continued singing my homemade scripture melodies aloud and baking my cookies. For there is one thing that I know, and it is that the devil hates scripture, and I like homemade cookies. So sing it was.

I knew that I was saved, and now God was going to save me from my own self-destructive mind. Hallelujah.

Tainted Windows of the Soul

Imagine a huge shell of a house with several windows built into it. Imagine that that house is your soul, and each window that you look out of has a different story to be told. You look out one window, and it is long and rectangular with a green tinge, while if you step just a few feet over, you can look out yet another completely different shaped window. This one is perfectly square and slightly grey-tinted. As you look, there is another window above you. If you look out that window and it casts everything in a kind of rosy color.

This house represents your tainted soul. Each one of these windows represents portions of your life. As issues have occurred in your life, as an abuse victim, the windows to your soul have become tainted. You look at life from your perspective, which has become slightly skewed. God began to show me that the way in which abuse victims look at life through the tainted windows of their soul is a lot different than, say, a person who has lived a Cinderella life.

Let me give you another example. Say that you were sexually abused by a father figure in your life; when you see a father giving affection to their young child, you as an abuse victim automatically, most times jump to the assumption that it is unnatural for a daddy figure to be giving that child such positive affirmations. That poor father figure becomes suspect in your eyes. From the eyes of the soul, your perception of life is somewhat warped from the perception that God created you to walk in.

Your purity has been robbed. Being sexually molested robs you of this purity. Once these repressed memories surfaced through dreams, I began to struggle with a sense of impurity. A sense of filth. The windows of my soul were tainting. The reason that I had a hard time going out into public was that I felt nasty; I felt dirty, and I felt used. Skanky. I felt like people could look in and see all that was going on in my soul. I felt unsafe, and I felt like nobody cared.

My trust factor for others was in an all-time low. I sure was not going to tell them what had happened to me. In the nineties, the media, newspapers, and the public arena were saying that repressed memory did not really happen, and so you could not really tell people about having repressed memories of being sexually molested. It's not like I wanted to talk to strangers; I'm not saying that. Yet I was finding this newfound freedom, and I just wanted to yell and tell people, "Now I understand why I have felt so filthy all these years."

People acted like they cared with a smile, but their ears were closed to listening. A little fake smile was all they offered, not wanting to burst their own happy bubble.

I had walked around with this feeling of filth for as far back as I could remember, and I could never understand what it was connected to. I walked around as if I was just sexually raped. I had been raped at twelve years old by a stepbrother, and yet I remember this feeling way before then. How did I know what that was like? Because, to my knowledge, before my memories returned, I should not have known before the age of twelve. And how did I know not to tell that this stepbrother had raped me? I was groomed to not tell. When it came to light, I realized that the only way that I could get rid of that impure feeling that I carried, that nasty, almost smelly feeling that was trying its best to hang around, was if I would verbalize the feelings; then, maybe they would leave.

When it first started and I was working full time as an agent, I would literally, without any exaggeration, get dressed in the morning, showered up, and get clean, fresh clothes, I was a perfectionist, and by the time that lunch-time came around, I would be in the office having to work the computers, the phones, and everything, and I would have to come home desperately feeling the need to change. The reason that I would change was that I felt dirty, the same feelings that I felt after being raped.

What happens when you are molested is that that Pedi touches you, and when they are done touching you, their body odor and their perspiration are left on your body. Often when I would be molested as a child, I either took a bath or showered immediately afterward, trying profusely to get the smell of the Pedi off of me. Into my adulthood, if even the mere accidental rubbing or touching by another male subject would occur, it would make me feel like I needed to go shower to get it off me. Sad. No handshaking here. I would not do my hair or makeup ever again. I would just get in the bath and wash my body and put new clothes on because the clothes I had on felt dirty and defiled. I would go back to doing whatever real estate I had to do; by the time I was done by three or four o'clock, I would have to go straight to my room to get changed. Boy, did I go through some fabric softener. I felt dirty. It was the most bizarre experience, and along with that came all this *anxiety*.

That is what happens where Satan has you so bound in the tainting of the windows of your soul. It is a process, and the deeper that you have been *bound,* the more your perception is *skewed*. You have no freedom in your body. You give up what little bit of freedom that you had, surrendering it to a strange sort of paranoia. You begin to think that everyone around you can *smell* you. That you are defiled goods, and all of this, of course, is just in your head, the doctors will tell you. Well, then why does it feel so real? Why is my laundry piling up by the boatloads?

Out the window goes your purity, one of those tainted windows. One of those windows that you feel like just jumping out of instead of facing the reality of what has happened to you. There is no way to get that purity back, and that is a sad thing. I guess that was some of my sorrow. Some of the pain of what I was going through is that I knew that I had had my purity robbed from me, and I never could understand how my husband and I were ever close. Supernatural. We were in love. We were passionate about one another, but there was always this screen there, and we could never seem to break through it. I had to come to terms and accept that this may always be that way. Screened in.

That is what my doctor explained to me. Something was stolen from me, and it was *pretty much lost*. I had to pick up the pieces that I *had left* and do the best that I could with what I had to quit looking back and trying to recapture something that had already been taken. It is like somebody stealing money from you. You knew that you had the money sitting right there, and you come back, and half of it is gone, and you cannot find it anywhere. You look everywhere, but it is gone. Someone has taken it from you, and that is the same with purity when impurity sets in. A tainted window. Something was stolen from me, and it was pretty much lost, and I just needed to deal with it.

Even in the writing of this right now, in my very skin, I just want to jump in the car and go shopping. You know, like the kind of shopping that makes you *feel good*. Where you can touch fresh, clean blankets, and the fur on the blankets feels so good against your skin. Clean, soft, and pure. Back to writing the book.

I still struggle with moments where I want to escape the pain that was inflicted upon me by my violator. This is where the sense of being defiled crashes up over your whole being. Abused. Sexually abused and stolen from. It is a very deep thing to go through. I am not here to say that you can never get it back because I do believe that God can heal and restore your mind from all of the defective and dramatic scenarios that warp your sense of life itself. But as far as the *actual purity*, it is lost. Just like the money was lost. I think that when I realized that, in the very beginning of the repressed memories, my purity had been stolen from me and that there was nothing that I could do to get it back, that was the beginning of the fuel to my fire. If I could not get my purity back, why should my Pedi have the freedom that he had? None of it seemed fair. Going through all of this is what made me determined that I was going after him. I do not want him to steal one little girl's purity away from her. No more loss. Enough already!

False Indoctrination

At the core of every child who has been abused is a lie. A lie told to that child, usually by an adult child (who was abused as a child) who was told the same lie. Unraveling these lies can be quite taxing, but through Christ, it can be done. It is interesting to me how very similar child abuse and false indoctrination are. Both must be stripped down to the very core of the lie that it has been built on in order for deliverance to take place. Both begin with a lie that mimics the truth and yet is still a lie. Both are placed into action by Satan. Both have an ultimate goal to destroy whomever and whatever comes in their way. Both increase into a form of brainwashing when done repeatedly. Repetition. Both connect themselves to legalism to be of any real power. Both are severely destructive to the soul. The soul becomes tainted. The windows to your soul or looking out from your soul because that is what we do, become cloudy and clouded with deception. Both keep a person in bondage to self, and *both take away your freedom of expression.* Both are debilitating to one's authentic expression for God and to God. The devil's ultimate goal. Both stunt your spiritual growth toward the knowing of heaven and our heavenly Father.

My experience has been that the only thing that could break through either one of them was time in the Word of God and seeking the truth of God.

Suffering a childhood of abuse is flat-out excruciatingly painful. Looking through the tainted defective windowpanes of my soul became more and more difficult as I grew older. It usually does not get any easier. Typically, a person who has endured living through sexual childhood abuse tends to take on a number of character defects that can take years to swim through; ultimately, though, you must allow God to reshape, remold, and rebirth who you were meant to be in order to become whole. Clean up on aisle seven.

Let me elaborate in further detail: While you were born with a certain personality, different defects begin pressing in and on to your character. With false indoctrination, it is the exact same process. Say that a girl was told that she was not very smart as a child. Say that girl internalizes those comments that were spoken to her; every time that she was told that she was not very smart, it was said to her in a different way. "You are not too bright," or "You are a terrible speller." Or "You will never amount to anything if you do not go to college. You do not study enough. What is wrong with you, dummy?" There were multiple ways that she heard that she just was not smart. Each way in which she heard that she is not smart affected her in different ways of her life. But they each affected her character in every facet. Slowly chipping away.

All that parent needed to do was be real with the child. The parent's unresolved fear ends up being passed down to that child. Realness would be for that parent to say to their child, "I really would love to see you create better study habits. What can I do to help? What do you need?" However, because the parents have never dealt with their own fears, their own pain, and instead have carried them throughout their life, the child ends up carrying the parents' fears for them, something the child is ill-prepared to handle, ultimately becoming a caretaker to the parents' feeling. Depending on that child's personality, they can react in a few different ways.

For me, I allowed it to taint my soul and become dark. One can become slothful and, in turn, become an even worse studier. Or one could become OCD about studying. Obsessive. Both are unhealthy. Both breed insecurities to future generations to come. I chose the latter.

So one would ask, at what point is one accountable to clean up the windows of their soul? To deal with their own fears. I say at the point that a person gets born again and accepts Jesus as their Lord and Savior, at that point where their spiritual eyes are opened, they become responsible to make right any *wrongs*, even ones perpetrated against you like child abuse...*right.*

Escalating Depression

The depression that I was suffering from was really beginning to escalate. After all, doesn't every commonsense psychologist teach you that depression is *anger* turn inward? Boy, did I have a right to be angry.

I would read the scripture, *"Rejoice not against me, O my enemy: when I fall, I shall arise; when I sit in darkness, the Lord shall be a light unto me"* (Micah 7:8).

I knew that this journey to healing was going to take some time because of the *"word"* that God had spoken to me and the detail of it. I equated it to a time in my young childhood when I had been severely burnt, and it took many, many months for the healing of my melted body to complete itself. There was *no less wait* put upon this issue. So time it was. What I did not realize was that it would take twenty years.

What I would like to explain to you and many people are not aware of is that a person does not just begin taking antidepressants with no side effects. What happened to me (and everyone is different) was that the antidepressants slowed me down. They physically caused me to move my body slower. I did not like this effect. A week into using antidepressants, I almost threw the entire prescription away. I almost turned back. I knew that God was using this medication; while some may say as a crutch, I say it was like having a *seeing guide dog* alongside of me. While I was blinded in this area of repressed memory for so many years, God placed this guide dog alongside of me, a.k.a. antidepressants, to help lead me down the road, down into my soul, toward divine healing.

I would cry out to God, trying to justify my explanations as to all that I was losing. I had lost my career. I felt like I was losing the emotional connection in my marriage. I had lost my social life, and still, God did not budge. Shocker.

He would come back at me with, "Do you want to lose your mind, or do you want to save your mind?" I know this is heavy for a lot of people, but it was the truth and how it was. It may seem deep that I talk to God in such a friendship-type communication, but I always have. Antidepressants became my friend. I had a choice. I could be mad and angry about what I felt that I was losing, or I could jump on the God bandwagon and accept what He had spoken to me. Give up the tough exterior and let God lead. I chose the latter. Even in my pain, God was softening, reshaping, and molding me. What a lot of people do not understand is that for the first several months when taking antidepressants, your body hurts. Your muscles ache. Your equilibrium is somewhat affected. You feel like somebody has run over you with your own *big ol' 350 truck.*

On the other hand, your body goes through a point of relaxation that I particularly had a hard time accepting. I wanted to fight it. That was not working for me. I do not profess to be a doctor nor to claim any diagnostics here, but I ended up using antidepressants for just about twenty years. I took them faithfully exactly as prescribed for the first eighteen years. It was only the last two years that the healing had been completed in me, and it was time for me to get off the antidepressants. I began to reduce myself and the milligrams that I was taking down till *nada.* You can read more about this in *Hollow Family Tree.*

Lonely Nights

With my husband gone many nights at a time, I just needed God to remind me of who He was and that He could keep me safe and was still in control. During these lonely, desperate long nights, I was living out each violation in my mind and, yes, crying in my soul. How could I overwhelm my husband any more than I already was with my personal pain? He saw me struggling, well as much as I would allow for him to see, and he had not a clue how to help me. He was not fully aware of how deep of a depression I had sunken into, as I had hidden as much of it from him as I could. I was embarrassed about how unable I was, beginning to *not* function. That is what primary caretakers do in times of crisis. I was in full-blown crisis mode. I felt forsaken.

In this time of financial crisis, while my husband was picking up as much overtime as he could and still giving emotionally during any of his infrequent home time, I was like a dry sponge needing more and more of what he had less and less of to give to me. Sucking. I knew that he could not fix me, but he would try his best to plug any holes up that he could to try and keep me from sinking. It was one vicious cycle that I am thankful now years later that I no longer must go through.

In the night times when I would be left home alone, as my husband was working, I was dealing with a lot of abandonment issues. Or so my doctor explained to me. What I caught myself doing was miss transposing the mere fact that he had to work and hold a job down and be gone through the night. He was a shift worker, and this had nothing to do with any deliberate plot on his part. There goes that paranoia again, imagining that he did not want to be around me because I was damaged goods. He loved me, and I loved him, but let us face it, it was my job to seek out the face of God. My husband had not forsaken me. It was not his job to fix me.

Quinceanera Rescuer

My daughter, now fifteen years old, would often come to my rescue. She would arrive home from school and see that I had *not* done a single personal thing for myself. She would urge me to jump into the shower, and when I got out, she would promise to help me to do my hair. Again.

Sad. A teenager should not be taking care of her mother. It should be the other way around.

It would go like this. I would have a memory, and immediately for days, I would want to shower or bathe two to three times a day. Two weeks later, I would only retreat to my room and sulk and cry and cry with no sense of control. I was all over the page of destitute. I needed to prevail. I will prevail. I felt guilty that I used my daughter for an ear to hear, but I was in such desperation and struggling with a lack of trust towards others that she was the one person that I did trust with my whole heart.

> *I will bear the indignation of the Lord, because I have sinned against him, until he plead my cause, and execute judgement for me: he will bring me forth to the light, and I shall behold his righteousness.*
>
> Micah 7:9

Vile Memories

Hanging onto all these vile memories was not why God *unrepressed* them for me. Holding on to them and not surrendering them and their pain was causing me to sin. Yes, sin. God released them to me through my memories for me to surrender them over to Him. You see, God wants all of us. He wants all of me. He wants us to go to Him and pour out our hearts. He cares for us and for our feelings. God loved me, and I knew this because He had so generously poured out His love onto me. I began pouring myself back out to God, telling Him of the pain that I would experience each time that He would bring another memory to my forefront. As I would do this, God would release me from any additional hatred and edginess I was suffering from toward my Pedi. Each memory I had begun surrendering over to God. Holding on to the hatred only darkens your soul. I was dealing with enough darkness as it was. God was going to *bring me forth. Propel me forth* so that I could and would behold His righteousness out of extremely dark circumstances.

> *Then she that is mine enemy shall see it, and shame shall cover her which said unto me, Where is the Lord thy God? mine eyes shall behold her: now shall she be trodden down as the mire of the streets. In the day that thy walls are to be built, in that day shall the decree be far removed. In that day also he shall come even to thee from Assyria, and from the fortified cities, and from the fortress even to the river, and from sea to sea, and from mountain to mountain. Notwithstanding the land shall be desolate because of them that dwell therein, for the fruit of their doings.*

> Micah 7:10–13

The walls that I built were built in darkness that came from a dark place in my life. For a season, they seemed to have protected me. God now wanted to break down those walls that were built from dark forces and build walls of protection that He built for righteous protection.

How come I was the one suffering still? The Pedi should have been the one in torment. After all, he was the atheist, the non-believer, and not me. It is kind of like how the drunk is not the one living in the pain because they are drunk all the time; it's the child that had to live in the parents' drunkenness that lives in the pain.

Nonetheless, my hope was and is in the Lord. God had to turn this around, and quickly if you ask me. Well, He turned it around, but it was on His timetable and not mine.

Detailed Dreams

I woke up with another one of those memories. God always seemed to speak to me in details. Detailed dreams. But these were more like vision dreams. In-depth descriptions of being violated by the Pedi. Painful. This daddy thing was being taken to a very ill level. This time he carried on as if he were having sex with his wife. I was eight years old. Daddy was not being so nice. He became violent in his efforts to try and get me to respond back to him. As if I were to love him back. He full-on raped me, violently and vigorously, sickly. He was mean and demeaning and aggravated that I would not voluntarily tell him how great he was or call him daddy. He became angry at my lack of submission. I resisted his sexual advances, and he became intensely agitated.

When he could not fully penetrate my young body, he stopped what he was trying to do and forced me to get on the telephone and call my older sister, who was at a friend's house. My sister refused to come home. Duh. She knew that he would try and rape her also. Angry with me that he had not completed what he had set out to do, he told me to just stay in my room as if I had done something wrong.

This memory was one of the most difficult to go through. Possibly because of the violence that he forced onto me and all the derogating comments that he spat out of his foul mouth. Violence.

Physical Evidence Dismissed

He had raped me. As each memory surfaced, I was little by little coming out of denial of what had been done to me as a young girl.

At this point, I saw it necessary to begin contacting my mom and asking her questions as to what she remembered. She at first thought that I was making up stories, as she put it, not telling the truth.

With each memory, as I explained the time, season, the given situation, the scene, the room, the weather, the clothes that he wore or didn't wear, the particulars of each event step by step, she came out of denial and began to remember.

When I recalled this memory of my Pedi raping me and told my mom about it twenty years later, she explained to me with much resistance that she remembered taking me to the doctor at or about this time. The doctor thought that I had been *harming myself* down there. He had found open cuts and abrasions in my private area. Really? Denial. Antibiotic prescribed. Quickly dismissed.

My mom's denial was so deep it nearly destroyed me as a child. I had done no such thing. I had been raped. Why couldn't she see? That should have been a CPS call. It was my way of *nonverbally* communicating, "Help! This man is harming me!" And then I would not have been to blame. You see, he was always trying to put the blame on somebody about something. That is what Pedis do.

"God is jealous, and the Lord revengeth; the Lord will take revenge on his adversaries, and He reserveth wrath for his enemies" (Nahum 1:2).

My stepfather had pulled me in on his family of origin's evil stronghold soul ties. He had pulled my mother in also. God was not happy about it. I was a child of God, appointed and anointed to preach the gospel. How dare this evil man used by Satan try to pull me into his slave of fear, addictions, and sins? God was and is abhorred.

"The Lord is slow to anger; and great in power and will not at all acquit the wicked: the Lord hath his ways in the whirlwind and in the storm, and the clouds are the dust of his feet" (Nahum 1:3).

So He will pay back good for evil. Make no mistake; God is slow to anger; however, He does get angry. God was angry at what my Pedi had done to me.

Crawling Worm

The memory of this sexual violation began working its way into my now existent life years later. My struggle with work was real. I began giving listings away just so I did not have to deal with people, *especially men*. When I would go into the public eye, fear was certain. Particularly if a man had facial hair, a split between their teeth, was built similar to my Pedi, or had a related demeanor. I felt like men could see right through my clothes. I would feel like I smelled. I would cry out to God for help.

"The Lord is good, a stronghold in the day of trouble; and he knoweth them that trust in him" (Nahum 1:7).

God began to put into my spirit that I needed to do something about it. I had held my secret oh so tightly as a child that now it was time as an adult to trust God and take His lead and come forth as God had instructed me to do. In the day of my trouble, which was now, God would be my stronghold. The darkness would pursue me no longer but instead would pursue my enemies.

"But with an overrunning flood He will make an utter end of the place thereof, and darkness shall pursue his enemies" (Nahum 1:8).

So even Satan hates his own self.

God showed me through His Word that these enemies would not bring darkness upon me a second time.

> *What do [you] imagine against the Lord? He will make an utter end: affliction shall not rise up a second time. For while they be folden together as thorns, and while they are drunken as drunkards, they shall be devoured as stubble fully dry.*
>
> Nahum 1:9–10

God was showing me that I would not have to suffer twice. I had already suffered enough. Although I was losing the ability to work as a real estate agent, it was not the end of me. He was going to deal with my drunken enemies. The Pedi must be exposed. If he were still actively touching, then exposing him would possibly help some other young girl from being molested. While I did not have proof deep within me, I knew better.

Was I up for this? There were days that I could barely function. How could I dare find any strength to do anything about it? *I could not...but God could.* If I were willing to be used by God, to be an instrument for God, He could start the process to stop this man that was bent on living in such evil.

God Who Hath

That thou mayest say to the prisoners, go forth; to them that are in darkness; Shew yourselves. They shall feed in the ways, and their pasture shall be in all high places. They shall not hunger nor thirst; neither shall the heat nor sun smite them: for he, that hath mercy on them shall lead them, even by the springs of water shall he guide them.

Isaiah 49:9–10

We serve a God who hath. Our God who has. Such an able God.

There is this fallacy that if you have been sexually abused, you will never fully measure up to receiving a full portion from the one who hath *all* to give. This is a lie straight from the pits of hell, for it is all yours for the taking. For even to Lazarus who was dead, Jesus spoke, "Lazarus, come forth."

Jesus speaks.

And he said unto him, Son, thou art ever with me, and all that I have is thine. It was meet that we should be merry, and be glad: for this thy brother was dead, and is alive again; and was lost and is found.

Luke 15:31–32

I was beginning to understand that God had never left me, even as the Pedi had violated me. He had allowed me to sleep for a season with the memories, but He had never left me. He is and was always with me. Even when I could not *feel* Him. He had allowed me to die off somewhat spiritually and a part of me to become stagnant for a while so that He could be the one who brought me back to life. So that I could truly know that God was with me and was within me. So that I would know Him and the power of His might. And that His power had raised me and *my mind from the dead.* Heavy truth.

"Finally, my brethren, be strong in the Lord, and in the power of His might" (Ephesians 6:10).

God was showing me that I needed to begin to walk in His power and the power that had raised me up. When God allows you to be persecuted— and yes, being sexually abused is just that—it is always for a reason. Do not ever let anyone tell you that God does not allow persecution to His people because the Bible teaches differently.

> *Blessed are ye, when men shall revile you, and persecute you, and shall say all manner of evil against you falsely, for my name sake. Rejoice, and be exceedingly glad: for great is your reward in heaven: for so persecuted they the prophets which were before you.*
>
> Matthew 5:11–12

Notice that it says that "when men shall speak all manner of evil against you..." This is exactly what a Pedi does to his victims. He tells you that nobody else will love you the way that he does and, in the same breath, says that no one will believe you and that nobody really cares about you. He may go as far as to tell you that you wanted *it* as much as he did. That is a lie. Possibly he may even tell you that you enjoyed it. All of this is a lie. My Pedi used to say, "Now, didn't that feel good?" Disgusting. The Pedi always breeds fear by using fear. So does Satan. Satan can't create, so he imitates, replicates, duplicates, and fakes anything that he does. So does the Pedi because the Pedi is controlled by the devil or his demons, possibly legions. If you were raised in a home where *lack prevailed* over much, the Pedi finds out what is important to you and tries to and oftentimes succeeds at using it to push you further back into the corner. You know that corner that you have become so comfortable standing in? That corner that on strong days you try desperately to get out of but never are able to obtain.

Family of Origin Reconciliation

While I was having memories surface, as if trying to live through that was not hard enough, also I was coming to terms with my emotions concerning my family of origin. This was a process that only the grace of God could have helped me in and through.

Letting go of sinful harbored hate held onto feelings was so *healthy* that it amazes me. Somehow, I felt a liberty to let it all go. Learning to love your non-Christian family of origin members after you have already left home is very soul searching. It is also so frustrating because I was not willing to give up my time to go back and iron out any unresolved issues, and there were a lot of them.

Not feeling loved by my mom made it even more difficult to want to even try to bring any sort of resolve. I needed God's power and help. Truly, I knew that if I did not put God in the middle of my family, my life, my problems, there was no way that I could even begin to cope with my past, my pain, or my childhood. Could I even make a difference as a believer? No, I could not. Only God could make that difference and quite possibly through me. So surrender was a must. It was *my must* for complete deliverance to take place. A step that I wrestled with profusely. While I am certain that had I known of how many years that this process would take for me and God to filter through, I would not have even tried to have approached the subject. So God, in His wisdom, took me step by step, day by day, until I got to the place of trusting Him enough to know that *He would not lead me where He Himself would not go.*

Eventually, I began to see my growth both spiritually and emotionally. Year by year, changes began to happen. Miracles began happening. I could not even begin to deny that the power of God was at work full time in my life. No part-time god for me.

You see, when you are sexually abused, a part of the brain emotionally stops maturing. Through the healing process, God had to take me back to where my growth was stunted and to begin to mend the pieces in my mind back together and raise me up to the point of maturity that I should have been at.

Could I come to a place of accepting my scars? "No, I do not think so," I would tell myself. Will I ever get there? How could I possibly? Did I ever end up with a closeness with either one of my parents? No, that did not happen either. You would think that God would have brought restoration after all the years of trials and prayers and reconciliation. He did in that He restored *me* out of it all. We *all* have free will. Your *free will* is released when you hand it over to God.

What God did do was pull me up out of the fire of destruction, and He placed me above on higher ground. He showed me that from my mother's womb, I was called to serve Him and that from the time of conception, God wanted me. This world may not have wanted me, my own mother may not have wanted me, but Jesus did. I was not a mistake. I was wanted by God. He began to show me that my journey was to be an example to as many people as He brings into my life. He blessed me with an honest heart, something that most are lacking. That honest heart led me to dig and dig and dig and pray and pray and pray until I got to the bottom of the darkened soul that I suffered from daily. Along the way to remembering all the sexual violations, He blessed me with scriptures and the presence of His being and Holy Spirit encounters, Jesus sightings, angel appearances, and times of worship that would last for hours upon hours. These are things that many Christians never even get the chance to enter into or experience, and for this, I am grateful. He showed me that I had a heart that wanted to know who He is, who He was, and who He is in me. He showed me that He gave me that heart from birth.

He is all power, all-knowing, all wisdom, all love, all peace, and all kindness. As God would show me yet one more facet of who He is, my faith was really beginning to grow, and my belief in God's power was increasing more and more. God's presence took up residency within me, and it was amazing.

"There is no fear in love; but perfect love casteth out fear: because fear hath torment. He that feareth is not made perfect in love" (1 John 4:18).

Where God's presence is, there is joy. Joy infects a person. Joy destroys fear and darkness and evil. Joy is the antidote that the world is longing for but does not even know it.

As I took care of God's business, the business that He would speak to me to do, to speak, to say, to bless, to provide, to give, to encourage, to love others, and as I was obedient to the presence of God that was invading within me, He put everything else into order. But He required me to first obey.

Familia Overview

My father got saved. My grandpa got saved. My three children got saved. And my grandma made peace with God before she died. What more could I ask for? God had granted me a man of God who really loves me, all of me. God blessed me with a husband who is my friend for life. He blessed me with a smart man. A hard-working man. A man of integrity. A man of faith. A man of courage. My husband has stuck by my side through thick and thin. He believes in me as a woman of God who hears from God and who believes that she is called of God with a purpose. He understands the need in me that must have time in her life to spend with God. He is willing to share me with God and to take second place. He understands that I put God first and then him. Now that is a very secure man.

My husband has not once questioned my motives. At first, he did question my memories, but with that admission of a phone call, he quickly knew I was remembering the truth. He knows that my motives are pure. He knows me. He knew me before I got saved, and he saw the dramatic change within me when I became converted for Jesus. He understood my hurting heart. He has watched me be molded and recreated by Christ, and he has watched me struggle with much pain and sadness when I have been betrayed and let down by my family of origin. He has watched me grow into a wonderful woman of God when it would have seemed easier for me to just give up. He has heard me weeping in the wee of the night, and he still loved me.

God took me from being concerned about feeling loved and all the steps that I tried to take to procure that love from my *family of origin* to centering in on my *nuclear family* that God had so graciously granted me with. My daughter, my two sons, my husband, and my beautiful eleven grandchildren. Not to mention the body of Christ. God gave me a love for my husband that is so deep and so pure. He allowed the both of us to be a fine example to the Christian community in several different states throughout the time of our marriage.

He taught me really early on within the first month of my salvation that if I was going to be a tither, in doing so, God would rebuke the devourer.

> *And I will rebuke the devourer for your sakes, and he shall not destroy the fruits of your ground; neither shall your vine cast her fruit before the time in the field, saith the Lord of hosts. And all nations shall call you blessed: for ye shall be a delightsome land, saith the Lord of hosts.*

> Malachi 3:11–12

God had increased my husband and me far greater than I ever would or could imagine being possible. God taught me early on to read His Word daily, take time out each day to worship, praise and seek and pray to the almighty Creator of the universe. What more could a girl ask for? He would speak to me that "It is not over until it is over." And He would say, "Who knows what relative will get resurrected next?" *He would say forgiveness flows in veins that are not clogged up.* He has taught me that my life is my testimony, and any opportunity that I must express God's love, God's healing, and God's Word, I needed to grab at it.

Nowadays, I try and find a way in any way possible to share the gospel with whoever it is that God causes to cross my path. I am not ashamed of my past, but I will be the first one to intercept if I see child abuse or child neglect happening because of my childhood. I have an ear to hear when an abused child is crying. I can see it written all over them. Had I not lived the childhood that I did and been healed, I probably would not be so in-tuned to the voice of one crying in the wilderness. Being untrapped by the power of God had helped me to *propel forward* to help others. When you are trapped in your own unhealthiness and sin, you do not have the tools nor the spiritual ability to help other victims. You must seek to become whole first. *In the seeking is where you are found.* That is just the way God operates. Kind of like the law of gravity...that is just how it works.

So my sin and past I keep under the blood. I have forgiven those who hate me and speak evil against me and continue to use me and be spiteful. I will continue to do so, as those people can and will cross my path because I have made a covenant with my God to never allow any one person to deposit hate or evil or discontent in or around me many years ago. My covenant with God is far more valuable than any emotion of *"dis"* that I could or should hang on to.

Keeping your covenants and vows is very important. There is nothing like being liberated from darkness and evil. I have found a newfound freedom in the forgiveness of others. It does not mean that you have to go hang out with *it* anymore, but it does mean that you are required to walk in the knowledge and love that God has given you. You cannot turn back; you must obey in order to obtain victory, keeping both hands on the plow. I have learned that it does affect the other person when we refuse to forgive them. It keeps chains around that person. I have watched repeatedly that when I forgive a person that I have *iced feelings* toward, it is then that God can and will deal with them, but forgiveness comes first. Unforgiveness hurts both the unforgiver and the one that you will not forgive. It is a two-way street.

Once my life was reconciled to the Lord and He began to pull me out of these dark memories, I decided that I wanted to be a Mary and not a Martha. I wanted to sit at the feet of Jesus even more than I already had been. Oh, how I enjoy my worship time, but I must do it with a pure heart. I must begin to try and forgive my Pedi.

I have learned how to handle rejection gracefully. Because the one who will never reject me is Jesus, and He is all that really matters anyways.

Even as the memories began to surface, I knew enough about the Word of God that as I started processing what had happened to me, God was already urging me to forgive. I was in a tug of war with God, saying, "Hey, can You let me process this first?"

The Holy Spirit was saying to me, "As each memory comes up, I want you to forgive..."

I began questioning God, "What do You mean as each memory comes up? Is there more?"

And God said, "Yes, there is more. I am going to show you more."

It was already becoming difficult to go to my mother with these memories; as I have said before, we were never close, nor would we ever probably be close. But for this time and period in my life, I was tabling my feelings because I needed validation of specifics to confirm my newfound findings.

You see, I never cared for my mother, her values, her ways, her awkward, strange beliefs, or her embarrassing behaviors. They always seemed contrary to mine. It was always hard for me to believe that she birthed me. While I would continually button the top button of my blouse, she would unbutton hers as far down as she could get away with it, constantly trying to lure people in sexually.

At this time when these memories surfaced in my life, my mom was at the depths of her alcoholism. She would come to visit about mid-way through my new memories and stay the night. She would crash on my couch with her hidden bottle of brandy that she kept tucked in her purse, and like most alcoholics, they think that nobody knows it. They think that no one can see that they are buzzed, and they really truly think that they are getting away with it. Her altered behavior said it all.

I felt quite hypocritical in a way, using her to unlock what would be my final memories of this Pedi. That in itself is another issue. For now, at that point in my life, I needed her, and it appeared she was there for me as best as she could be.

God will even use your enemies to help you out. In my heart, my mom was my enemy. She hated God; she hated Christianity, so when I was around her, I was allowing my guard to come down in regard to the sexual molestations while at the same time keeping *my guard up* to protect my relationship between Jesus and me. Spiritual warfare at its peak.

With each new memory, my mom would pick it apart or try to pick apart what had happened to me. She would seek to try and catch me in a lie, trying desperately to prove that I was lying. I believe she was dealing with so much guilt that she had married this man. It would be easier for her if, in fact, none of this that was being exposed was the truth. I believe she was trying to relieve her guilt. Because somehow, it put a flashlight onto her and her alcoholism and the life that she had and was still actively living. While she never said as much, the way that she would gather up her belongings and go back to her home (because after all, she only had a drop or two left of that brandy that was tucked away in her purse) said it all. You would have just had to be there to fully understand her and her mannerisms...just saying. I despised the liquid drug called alcohol. It had played a part in far too many of the negligent abuses that I had endured.

The Unrowed Boat

Let us get back to what this book is really about, *repressed memory* and how it happens. Some time had passed, and I was still trying to regurgitate the first several dreams that I had had. I thought, *O Lord, You must be done; You must have shown it all to me*, knowing on the inside by this time that he had harmed me more times but hoping it was over. It is not something that I made happen; these dreams just came through the night. They were actual dreams that I had while I was sleeping. I woke up, and it was as clear as day. I would start freaking out as if it had just happened to me. Well, here came another dream.

This violation happened on a family camping trip with the Pedi's family of origin visiting from another state. While I had always remembered the camping trip, in this dream, I remembered an aluminum boat and how the Pedi lured me down to the lake, telling the family that he was going to teach me how to row a boat and that I was to meet him down at the water's edge. He did not walk with me to the water. He went and got the boat into the lake ahead of time. While I moseyed on down to the waterfront, I knew that he was up to no good.

He never wanted to spend time with me alone without an ulterior motive and definitely not in public. It was always behind closed doors. The one thing that was in common with all the molestations was that my mother was not anywhere to be seen, nor was she this time.

There he was in the boat, waving his finger at me to get into the boat. I stepped into the mucky edge of the water, the sooty mud coming up through my toes, and my heart went to the pit of my stomach. There was that same feeling as if I were the one doing something wrong. I couldn't stand to have dirt on any part of my body, and I remembered trying to get out of the boat but also rinse the dirt off of my feet so that when I got into the boat, I would have mud in my feet. The Pedi was annoyed like I needed to hurry up and just get in the boat; all the while, I was hoping that my mom would just come around this bend and rescue me. That did not happen.

As the boat left the shoreline, he wasted no time in letting his intentions be known...me being the obedient child, of course, obeyed. The good one. The perfect one, as he would call me, obeyed his commands. It was a quick violation, and before long, he had abruptly pulled up to the shoreline demanding harshly that I quit crying. Self-serving. I had begun crying as he went back to the shore. I guess he was not going to show me how to row a boat today. He told me to quit crying and shut my mouth and get back to the campground where I belonged. I got back out of the boat into the muddy water seeping into my toes, crying. He dismissed me and went back out onto the water by himself.

Bright and Early

The next morning after this dream, because I knew not to call my mom too early, I anxiously waited for the clock to strike twelve. Hangover. I asked her if she remembered the camping trip.

She replied snippily, "Yes, of course, I do." At this point, I had had four previous distinctive dreams, memories. So she was fully aware of what was coming next.

I proceeded to explain what had happened to me in this aluminum boat, to which she quickly denied ever even having a boat. She said, "Yes, we went camping. It was a family event. It was good quality time, and I don't understand the problem there."

I countered her defensiveness with, "He molested me in that boat."

"Well, that couldn't be possible," my mom spat out sarcastically. "We didn't have a boat; I told you."

But I was persistent because I knew what I had dreamt, and I knew what had happened because my body was reacting as if I had just been molested. The previous dreams acted in an identical way. I would have the dream, and my body would react as if I had just been molested. So I was going to get to the bottom of whose stinking aluminum boat it was.

"Did we rent the boat?" was my next probing question to my mom.

"No, we never rented a boat," was her sharp reply.

"Did we borrow the boat?"

"Absolutely not. We didn't borrow anything from anybody," she stated adamantly.

So I left the conversation that day saying, "Think about it, Mom. It happened. We can face this together," because I knew by the tone of her voice she was in full-force denial mode.

I hung up the phone that day, knowing just like the other dreams that it would probably take her a day or two, and she would be calling me back or showing up at my doorstep.

The next day, later in the afternoon, my phone rang, and it was my mom. She said, "I thought about that camping trip, and you were right; his brother and family who had accompanied us on the camping trip had an aluminum boat." She sounded defeated with a solidarity to her voice.

She said, "I am so sorry. I did not know. He really did molest you, didn't he?"

I said, "Yes, Mom. Yes, he did."

I hung up the phone, not having added much more to the conversation because I was hoping that it would maybe penetrate her.

My hope was that possibly she would realize that she had some accountability for her denial because her denial and her use of alcohol are what caused him to keep perpetrating these outrageous and despicable acts against me. The Pedi's malicious and oppressive intentions had been ignored by my mother. All the signs were there, and yet for some reason, she turned a blind eye. Role-playing. Devastating role-playing.

I guess it was time to get my pen and paper out again and document this last dream that I had had. In dreaming it, you go through it. When you document by writing it, you go through it yet again. And each time, the *shame base* piles itself up on top of you. The *shame base whispers* begin calling out to your mind accusing you the same way the Pedi did each time that he would molest you. Those *whispers* only repeat themselves, and that is how you know that they are not true. Just like I told you earlier, Satan cannot create; he can only imitate, replicate, and duplicate. Getting rid of the shame would take years, but for now, I would just document another dream.

Slipping Public Persona

Trying to keep up with the Joneses was slowly slipping away, though I would try. You see, I had gone to a cosmetology academy and graduated by age nineteen, so I had pretty much perfected the doing my hair, makeup thingy. Most days, I looked like I had it all together. I had learned how to fake it at a young age. Ha. Now with the antidepressants being fully ignited into my system, my daughter was able to take some much-needed time off from her codependent parenting schedule. The deep sunken depression that I had been in seemed to be lifting. Now, the anxiety I was living in was a different story. On a good day, I was now able to function at about fifty percent capacity. We will not mention on a bad day.

At this point, I tried of no volition to start taking a little bit of a turnaround of that bin. Public persona slipping more each day.

No Locked Doors Allowed

The final time that he molested me came through a dream also. We were never allowed to lock any doors as a child. As a matter of fact, back in the sixties, the only doors that came with locks on them were the bathroom door and your back and front door. It was forbidden to lock the bathroom door. You could get a whipping with a belt or get restricted to sitting on the edge of your bed for an hour. Rules were not to be broken in our house. And this was a strictly enforced house rule.

As I was in the shower, I thought that I heard the bathroom door open. The next thing that I knew, the Pedi was in the shower with me. It was as if he was saying goodbye in his sick way. He and my mom were soon to be divorcing, and in his very sick twisted way, he entered the shower like I owed him something for taking care of me for the past five years. I knew he was going to be leaving our home shortly. You could overhear the arguments constantly. He had endured back surgery, and it had been agreed upon that once he recovered, he was a goner. So he was just trying to fit in one last sick, perverted event. I told myself that this could be the last time, and then he would be out of here. Hopeful thinking.

While I called my mom and told her of another dream, I did not really need her validation at this point. I knew what I knew to be true.

Mustered Courage

Each morning when I would wake up, I would do my usual. Get my hot coffee, my legal-size notepad, and my Bible, and off I would go. I would read, pray, praise God, sing worship, think, read some more, and of course, journal.

This morning my mind went off like a light bulb, and I remembered the phone book. I started trying to recall the little girls that I had gone to school with as a young child or that lived in my neighborhood. In what I believe to be the prompting of the Holy Spirit, I took my legal notebook and my pen, and I started writing down all of the first and last names of the people that I could think of. I looked up as many *landline phone numbers* of every family that I thought might possibly have been affected. I came up with a list full of them.

Wow, what a small world. So many years later, and a huge portion of them still lived in Los Angeles County. Now I just had to muster up the courage to contact as many as possible.

I finished up my praying that day and waited for my daughter to get home from high school. While I knew that my daughter probably, from a counselor's viewpoint, was not the ideal person to enroll in this task, I knew that she would want to know what the latest of this scandal was. Yes, it appeared to me it was becoming a family scandal. There had been enough secrets in my family line that I wanted to be transparent with my newfound repressed memory issue.

One family stuck out for me like a sore thumb. I decided then and there to get up the nerve and make the call. Much to my surprise, the mother of this girl answered the phone. I identified myself, and she did not quite remember me, so I described in further detail where I lived, on what corner, and how her daughter used to babysit. I explained my dilemma with the repressed memory and filing the suit against my Pedi.

Amazingly, she admitted that at or around that time, when this could quite possibly have occurred, she and her daughter started having a lot of problems communicating. She stated that there very well could have been a possibility of her daughter having been molested, raped, attacked, or approached around this time. Sadly, she said that she really wouldn't have been able to find out any much-needed information because her daughter had gone into prostitution and that she wouldn't really have a way to contact her and hadn't been in contact with her for several years. Sadness.

My heart became grieved because I understood the finality of what I was doing placing these phone calls, and I very well understood the reality of emotionally separating one's self from pain.

We ended our conversation with the understanding that she would contact me if she were to happen to speak to her daughter, which periodically every few years she did. She encouraged me not to give up on my journey. I never heard from her again.

My daughter's jaw was dropped at the conclusion of this phone call. She said adamantly, "Mom, you have got to call them all."

I responded, "Not today." Phew. I had this confirmation that we were going down the right road here. It really threw me for a loop, draining all my energy. We would have to start up again tomorrow. My first hunch phone call would give me so much information; the feedback was shocking. I wanted to internalize my response of emotions, but I had internalized enough, so I verbalized my opinion instead. I was disgusted that this Pedi quite possibly harmed our babysitter. While these are unsubstantiated claims, and of course, we will keep the name anonymous, my Pedi knows who she is, and he knows what he did to her. You see, she was our babysitter, well she babysat us a few times. The way that these Pedis work is that they scope out the scene. That is probably why he did not do anything the first time that she babysat.

I believe my mother drove her home the first time. After all, she was on the payroll now, and so a *little supposed* trust had been built. The second and last time my Pedi drove her home, I thought that it was peculiar that he was going to drive her home. But he volunteered, and my mom let him. She just lived right down the street, and I remember thinking that it took him far too long to get back home. Being a victim of incest, you tend to pay attention to all the fine details.

When asked to babysit again, her mother flat out stated that she would not be returning to your house to babysit for my parents during their weekly bowling league night.

After that, Kathy and I babysat each other. They would not get home until close to ten o'clock at night. My mom would put my younger brother down to bed, and Kathy and I would stay up and watch *Ironside*, an old murder mystery series. It could get quite scary being home alone (imagining crazy things with no one there to tell you how to think), but it was what some dysfunctional parents did in the sixties.

The following day, I started in on my not-so-fun adventure with the white pages. One family that lived right down the street from us as kids, come to find out, was still in contact with my Pedi. Good friends, in fact. Boy, did I have to backpedal out of that conversation and quickly. The mother proceeded forth to kind of put me in my place and let me know how she thought that I was completely wrong about him, and I just needed to *put a smile on my face* and *quit digging up old bones* and *learn to be happy*. I am certain that she contacted the Pedi and let him know I was on his trail. She let me know that nothing happened to her children from my Pedi and that they were very well adjusted in society and doing well for themselves, and she asked if we would like to meet for lunch sometime in a facetious tone. That was not going to happen. As I remember it, they were kind of weird to begin with. On to the next one.

After this second phone call, I thought, *Okay, stop, enough is enough*. You are just imagining things. This is kind of how the mind works with both a repressed memory mixed in with a little dose of shame. I thought about it for two whole seconds, but I needed to do my *due diligence* if there were any more children out there that he had touched. More witnesses.

One of the names on the list was the Pedi's brother and wife. They lived in the local San Diego area. I called them and reached the wife, who would have been my step-aunt in my childhood days. I explained to her what he had done to me; she had two daughters. Interestingly enough, when the Pedi would talk about these two daughters, he had put them in two categories just like Kathy and me, one was the sweet, petite one, and one was the older, taller, more aggressive one. I explained to her about my concern, and she just kind of laughed it off and assured me that *he was a good uncle and would never have touched her daughters*, and if he had, *surely they would have told her*. But she agreed to meet with me, and a few weeks later, we did so but to no avail. She even brought one of the two now-grown daughters with her.

You see, while she was denying that he ever touched her daughters, she was curious as to what he had done to Kathy and me and why she was just now hearing about it. It did not take too many years from then that the Pedi's brother completely cut the Pedi off and quit talking to him for *an unspoken reason*. You can come to your own conclusion about that.

I continued reaching out and making phone calls, but I was never able to make contact with anyone else on my list. I felt that I did the best I could with the energy that I had to muster up to make those phone calls. Defeated.

The Other Sister

I was still in communication with my baby sister. She was the Pedi's real birth daughter. I had pretty much raised her the first six years of her life. We had a bond at the hip, and that was slowly being disconnected. You see, she was having a growing concern for her own self, her marriage, and her reputation. Understandably.

I had inquired what she thought about the possibility as to whether her Pedi dad had touched her baby sister. This was a sister born through the Pedi's second marriage. I even mentioned the possibility of him touching the granddaughter. Or any one of the many girl scouts under his wife's troop. She was also the director for the entire Simi Valley division.

My sister instantly and unequivocally denied it all. "He would not do that. He might have touched you, but he would not just go touching people randomly." *I guess I was random.* What a degrading comment.

She did, however, reluctantly admit that there was an incident during the one year in high school that she had decided that she would be better off living with her dad. One of her girlfriends said that something really weird and sexually inappropriate had happened with her dad coming on to her. Of course, this was just an *isolated incident,* and she *was not too concerned* about it. Really. We are talking about a sexual predator at this point and not just a Pedi. We have a problem. Unanswered concerns.

I quickly realized that my sister was in denial and desperately wanted to cover up for her dad's behaviors. I began to emotionally pull away from her, carefully and methodically. She was becoming sharp, rude, mouthy, and snippy.

At one point, I boldly stated, "Are you sure that he didn't molest you?"

She replied definitively, "Absolutely not! I would know if he molested me. He never molested me. He never touched me." While she appeared on the outside to be remorseful for her father's behaviors, and I believe that she somewhat was, she seemed more concerned with the impact to her own life as she was trying to climb the corporate ladder with her newfound position in the fast-paced LA lifestyle. How dare I have any feelings at all about this? How dare I think outside of the box that quite possibly could he have harmed her or other relatives?

Weight Gain

I learned from my doctor that when a child is molested, eventually even into adulthood, the inner child will fight back. They will demand a right to be a child. To live in purity. With no explanation.

From my youth, I enjoyed baking, so as an adult, I told myself that I could pray and bake my way through this. Here I go again; I would bake so much that I would have to freeze in Ziploc baggies, brownies, cookies, banana bread, and candies all at the same time. No joking. As my memories were becoming unfrozen, I was beginning to *feel*.

God is good. And His mercy endures forever. Man, oh man, did I need mercy (unmerited favor).

From the age of about eleven to twenty-two, I was either anorexic or bulimic or a combination of the two. I would throw up my food anywhere from one to three times a day depending on the circumstances and who either was or was not around. I am certain that this is in direct correlation to being both molested by my Pedi and raped by my stepbrother. No doubt. In bulimia, I learned to chew my food well. It's caloric manipulation 101.

This took such a toll on my body, my throat, my health, and my attitude. It is almost slightly manic and euphoric. I would feel an urgency to go throw up all I had eaten. The addictive cycle is just that, addictive. I could not just stop. I would throw up in a sink. I would throw up in a toilet. I would throw up in a shower. I would throw up in just about any place that I could to get that food out of me. I would use my fingers to throw up with, and yet I would stick my fingers down the drain to unclog it to get the food to go down it. Quickly. Manically. So that I did not get caught. During that euphoric time, *all morals are sacrificed*. Base lined. Frenzy.

When I became a Christian at age twenty-two, all throwing up and starvation stopped. What did not stop was the weight management programs in my head. Somehow, I had figured out that I was most comfortable with very little fat on my body. At this time in my life, what I was going through in my newfound memories, I began to find comfort in food and comfort with a lil fat on my body as well. While I was still in weekly therapy, living in the pain of being sexually molested proved to be very difficult. The evidence was starting to show in my hips.

I was playing sports four to five nights a week. With all of this past being kicked up in my life, I was having a difficult time going out into public. One by one, I quit all the softball teams that I was juggling so manically to play. Metabolism halt.

While I no longer had the metabolic increase nor the adrenaline rush that I received from being active on the baseball teams, I also no longer saw 150 on the scale. I had always strived to perfection to keep my weight under this mark. When I hit the 155 mark, I would cut a meal out of my daily eating routine. At five foot seven, I did not look too bad for my age, but that 150 went to 185 in no time. All the sitting around, depression, and lying around were beginning to take a noticeable toll on my body. I went from a size twelve to a sixteen within six months of remembering the sexual violations that were done against my body. It was nothing that I did on purpose. It just happened. Eating was becoming a comfort for the first time. Yeeha.

I had a disconnect with food that had started at a really young age, as far back as age four and a half, when I was hospitalized with severe burns covering a large portion of my small body. I was forced to live off an IV for food. Food disconnection. Add to the equation that I lived with a mother who believed that if you were not counting your calories, then she was counting them for you. In conjunction to her counting your calories, she was counting the pennies and dollars as well as verbalizing that it was costing her too much money to feed you, and she let you know as such.

Consequently, at a very young age, I began to sneak food. That wasn't too hard to do as my mom was either getting ready to have a drink, had had a drink, was working on more to drink, or passed out with dinner simmering on the stove when I arrived home from school. This is a common habit of a bulimic.

Along with all of this began certain phobias of foods that I carried with me and still do. Comments like, "Do you know how many calories are in that slice of bread?" Do not even mention potatoes, which were pretty much banned from our diet. I take responsibility now as a mature adult for my food issues. But the beast that was created in me, now...that is a whole other book.

I had come to the point at this time in my life that I had enough issues, problems, etc., not to mention my three wild and rebellious teenagers that counting calories got pushed on to the back burner. When I breached the subject to my therapist about this encroaching problem of weight gain during one of my grueling sessions, he stated, "Let us not worry about that, Cynthia. You have far more pressing issues at hand in your life to be concerned with." I guess he was right.

By the time I got through all the court issues, I had learned to truly enjoy a well-rounded meal, all 237 pounds of me.

One of my counselors actually encouraged me to begin dealing with my inner child issues. Another subject to write about. He stated that "If you want to order two hamburgers, then go for it. One for you and one for your inner child." Nuts. Though this train of thought had some merits, it was not helpful to my rear end or my dwindling pocketbook.

The average person finds vices to help them cope with these heavy issues. My own personal convictions would not allow for a glass of wine to numb with at the end of a hard day. But that chocolate chip cookie seemed to suffice and do the trick for me. Numbing at its worst.

Public Arena No More

One of the hardest phobias for me to overcome has been going into public places. I felt nude at times. Literally nude. Cornered at times. And trapped at times. Anytime I was in public. And I definitely had a hard time going into public if I was alone.

My counselor explained to me that most of this was in my head. While it was good to pay attention to everything that was going on around you, she felt that I was taking it to the extreme.

I can guarantee you that this counselor was never sexually molested. It would not take me too much longer for that counselor to do a forward lateral and hand me off to one of her partners. She was what you would call a clinical psychologist. In other words, they have not experienced what you are going through. They have only learned in clinics or courses how to supposedly handle it with patients.

The emotions and experiences that I was having were real, raw, and affecting me as I was walking through them. Being in public alone became a *no-no*. While I would be forced to be in a predicament to be alone such as going to my counseling sessions, carpool, there were no single trips to the grocery store on my watch if I could avoid it.

There were days when I intended fully on going to do something. I would get up, makeup, hair, ready to walk out of the door, and *fear* would stop me dead in my tracks, changing my mind. My family graciously adjusted too many halted or delayed plans during this time. Anxiety was trying quickly to befriend me. When you have lost most of the public interaction that you had entertained for the past ten years, anxiety did not seem to be such a bad friend after all. At least I had a friend. Head-trips. After all, I had lost most all my friends. They could not seem to handle what I was going through. So most of them pulled away. The friend I needed most was my baby sister, but she went basically AWOL. Gone. Abandonment hurt, but I understood, as she chose a side, and it was the Pedi's side, not mine. Painful.

What Is Repressed Memory?

Repressed memory is like being in a closet for thirty years and all of the sudden having someone crack the door open, but just slightly. You have reversed reactions. Joy for the light to come in, fear for the pain that the light causes. But if the door never gets opened, you are always in the dark.

For example, when you give birth to a baby and they stitch you up, and then they have you use a sun lamp to dry out the stitches. The light is hot and hurts, yet without the light, if you were to remain in those stitches, then you remain in a dark, damp environment, and there would be no healing. If I were to have remained in darkness, I would still be in a silent inferno for the rest of my life.

Phobias, fears, and frights. To enter into denial is more painful at first, but ultimately, healing does come. When light or truth began shining into my closet, it hurt. I was fearful. It was as if the blindfold was removed from my eyes. One way I can explain is like this. Say the police are going to take you to a rape scene. They *blindfold you,* and they drive you to the scene, and it takes hours to get to the scene. All of a sudden, the car stops, and you can hear the police get out, and you can hear the door slamming and opening, preparing to get you out of the car. The policeman grabs ahold of your hand very aggressively, and he walks you to the scene. He removes your *blindfold* abruptly, and you see that it is *you lying there* raped and crying, sad and lonely and in despair. You can see that *it is you,* but you cannot believe that it is you. *But it is you.* It is you. It definitely is you. It has happened to you, no doubt. It is you. You do not want to believe it, but what choice do you have? Scared and fearful, you want to go back into the *blindfold* and remain in denial forever. After all, didn't that feel safer? The pain coming onto you in the light seems more painful than when the blindfold was on. Fast forward.

A few years go by, and the pain of the memories is still excruciating. So severe that nobody can really understand. Nobody. They all just sympathize and shake their heads as if they understand, and yet they do not. You just want to die.

At this point, that seems the only way to escape the pain. For me, swimming through the pain with no drug-induced feeling was very hard. I had been clean and sober for over fifteen years. I do not know if I am so proud of that or not. It has been horribly painful. Somedays, I felt like doing something drastic, but I knew that I would regret it. Plus, my children look up to me, and I must set an example not to be a hypocrite to them. So I will try my best to be a good person.

Honest, truthful, drug-free, alcohol-free. Not to kill, steal, or destroy. High moral standards.

Mommy Dearest

Like I said earlier, I was at a point in my life that I had sworn I would never come to. I needed my mother's memories. I guess you could say, if I am being perfectly honest, that I used her. Because I did not like her, and I did not respect her. When I say that I did not like her, I mean I did not like her personality. In general, I do not care for that type of personality in any person, not just because she was my mother. That is just not the personality type that I am drawn to. She is the cup half empty kind of gal, agnostic some days, neurotic, extra centrically aggressive, and verbally abusing anyone that she encounters. I did not look forward to going into public with her and avoided it at all costs. She had embarrassed me far too many times in my life. Why would she start to make a change now? So to say that I felt guilty for using her just to get to the bottom of her memory bucket is putting it lightly.

This being the most vulnerable part of my life, she was by far the last person I felt safe being defenseless around. Her insensitivity stung deeply, and the wound would last for days when I was vulnerable; just one conversation with her could be so rude and intrusive and derogatory. That, you would have had to have an encounter with her to understand. It is as bad as I am telling you. The last person I wanted to *share* with.

At one point, my counselor tried pushing me into a *share group* with my mom. She acted as if it would be helpful. That was not happening. Then she recommended a *share group* with strangers. As if it was an honor to be selected for it. Not going to happen either. Not even remotely close to what I needed. She did not get me.

One definitive fact was that my mom hated and despised Christians. With these repressed memories, I was very forceful and boisterous that God had given me back these memories through dreams. I had decided out of emotional desperation that I was not going to put up with her baloney any longer. She carried a hate for this ex-Pedi stepfather of mine, and she was very willing to jump on the hate bandwagon with all this new information that was coming to light. She could not handle or stand being around me any more than I could handle or stand being around her.

With each new dream, I would confront her for validation of facts, and I could see the evil that was within her thriving and growing like I was feeding it. You see, she was never able to get revenge for him molesting my older sister, which she knew about. So now it was kind of a filthy blood-bonding bath for the two of us. I knew that it was wrong, but I needed her memories and had no other source but my older sister, who was becoming less and less reliable by the minute. I could sense that there was a healing that God wanted to do, start, and continue within my mother with regards to the failed marriage that she had with this Pedi. But that was not my concern currently, nor had it ever been because it is not my life. That was not my story. That was not my issue. I had to come to the point that I had to take care of myself no matter what her agenda was in the situation. I did not respect my mother for staying married to this Pedi for five grueling years, and I certainly wasn't going to have any form of conversation with her in regard to the Pedi unless it added and assisted in my case against him. To this, I was living in my truth.

We tried to bond on a very dysfunctional level. We would watch the OJ Simpson trial of the nineties and get on the phone and discuss what Judge Edo had done that day. Once that trial was done, along came the Lorena Bobbitt trial, and that was more up my alley.

It was not that we both did not try; it was just dead from the start. You see, I was secretly given up to my grandmother for the first three years of my life, a fact that was sickly covered up as I grew older. Even to the point where she boisterously claimed to have breastfed me. I kept digging and digging, trying to figure out why there was no bond there between mother and daughter to no avail. No connection found. While I do respect her for going out of her comfort zone to try and assist me with what she did remember, I always knew that she had a hidden agenda, or so she thought. It was not so hidden to me.

She actually weakened my case against the Pedi because the information that she and I would discuss, unbeknownst to me at the time, would get leaked to my baby sister, the Pedi's daughter, and would bleed back to the Pedi. If that's not dysfunction and betrayal, then I do not know what is. If that is what somebody calls love, then I do not want it. Not interested.

Kathy, Kathy, Kathy

While I respected my older sister, Kathy, for relocating down to the San Diego area closer to me, I would be a fool to not acknowledge that she had a severely debilitating drug problem that was not going away any time soon. When she first relocated, for a short period, she kept in good contact with me. With the best of intentions, she was trying to be there as a sister with a high failure rate. Kathy had her own fears to wrestle with. Through all the muddy waters that I was swimming in, it became very apparent to me that I had also taken on the role of *the rescuer*. In a family of dysfunction, particularly when there are addicts involved, everybody plays a part. Role-playing.

I was quickly becoming aware of just what my character role was in this long line of dysfunction. I was the *rescuer, the fixer, the refiner,* if you might say. I was good at pretending, trying to make everything perfect, clean, neat, tidy, and not undone. She was the *scapegoat.* The *black sheep.* The *dark one* as the Pedi tried to make her out to be. He had pitted the two of us against one another. He had planted suggestive thoughts about her to me and vice versa. She thought of me as being the favorite. "You were a good girl, and you deserve pretty things. If we aren't friends, then he wins," she once said to me. He used to tell her that I was Ms. Perfect, Ms. Clean, Ms. Orderly, and Ms. Judgmental, and she was bad news. From my perspective, he made her out to be something that no one would want to be involved with. She was a bad person and a liar. Twisted mind games.

So, as I was trying to deal with these issues of molestations, my sister and I could not seem to find any real common ground, and boy did we try. We were contrary to one another. She was a street prostitute and crack user, living a very foul life and trying her best to run away from her life, feelings, and emotions. Here I was, a strait-laced Jesus lover, family-oriented, Ms. Prim and

Proper, trying my best to get into touch with my emotions and memories. We were worlds apart. How could this breach ever be filled? God alone knew.

I remember before the Pedi came on the scene that we would help each other pack our lunches for school when our drunken passed-out mother was in the other room. If we had a nickel, we would buy a Popsicle from the Popsicle man. We would break the Popsicle in half and share it fifty-fifty. Now that is love.

On Sundays, if we had managed to get approval from our drunken mother the day before, we would go out and stand on the front street corner and wait for the periwinkle-colored church bus to come pick us up and take us to Sunday school at a church that my mother and father had shortly attended before their divorce. Could I ever reclaim ownership in that sisterhood friendship that was so evilly tainted? Little did I know at that time that that was not going to be attained until twenty years later. So many tainted windows.

There were many scenarios that occurred in the next several years in trying to rescue my sister and our relationship. Let us not forget, after all, that was my role. It was a cycle of rescue, repair, fix, and relapse. Her cycle was to use, to get, to take advantage of, and to then escape back into the environment that was most comfortable for her lifestyle.

One occasion, when I tried to pick her up off the streets, was very memorable. The time when I almost found myself arrested. With my fine, freshly waxed car, I attempted to get her to come home with me one day. The police were sure that I was her pimp. I found myself digging frantically for one of my real estate cards, all the while assuring the officer that she was my sister. My husband assisted me in driving that day; he was not happy. Through much convincing, the officer finally relented and allowed her to get in my car if I would leave the area immediately. You see, just as I was showing up to pick her up from the streets, it just so happened that she was in the middle of being arrested for public intoxication and a nuisance. It took all that I had in me to not just drive away as the officer was encouraging me to do. Instead, I stood my ground, fighting for her to get in my car and leave with me that day.

This was just one of the numerous times of rescuing. Possibly I felt that if I could just get out of my own head for two seconds with all my problems of this *repressed memory stuff*, I could somehow fix her and make her whole. There is only one who makes whole, and that is God alone, I soon discovered. I had my role-playing mixed up. My husband informed me that day that he was not doing it again. Ever.

As a family, we were hopeful. We all had such high hopes that Kathy would find sobriety and meaning for her life. My family would express a deep desire and concern for their aunt K to get clean and sober and on the right track. They would wait out arrivals anxiously and expectantly, hopeful that this would be the time she would really turn her life around. She was quite the character to be around once she would sober up. Quick to pull out her guitar and sing a soulful song as she strummed a few notes. She had a love for my kids and a yearning to know them and be a part of their lives. Yet, due to her heavy drug use, she found it difficult to connect with us for a sustainable period of time. Maybe it was that glimpse at the true love that fanned the flame of fear in her propelling her back to the streets. Oh, the misery of feeling and being lost.

Time and time again, she would call me on the phone, telling me how she wanted to get sober. Begging me for my help. Begging me to come down yet again and pick her up. Promising sobriety but oftentimes refusing treatment centers. Claiming that she could do it on her own. *Nada* was going to happen.

I would get her home to my house and get her bathed, cleaned up, and freshly clothed and wash what she had on, on a repeat cycle. Feed her and maybe even give her a haircut. And within four to five hours later, she was conning me into giving her a ride back to the streets. No rehab was in sight. Back to the streets, she would go. Solemn nights.

Dim Chances

While my legal case was ongoing, Kathy had gotten to the point where she did not even want to discuss it. Just the mere mention of the Pedi's name would send her in a thither. I knew by now that the district attorney had received all the legal documentation against this Pedi. While it was looking dim that we could prosecute the Pedi, there was still a glimmer of hope that we could get my sister cleaned up enough and long enough that she could be a *reliable witness* in what we hoped would be an upcoming trial. That did not happen.

She had been in and out of maybe five rehab programs, either being kicked out or leaving them in a short period of time that she had been in San Diego County. I still needed to try. My current attorney had secured an appointment with a Los Angeles County district attorney. She explained to me that if I could get my sister in my possession and get her cleaned up both physically and chemically, she and I could drive up to the heart of Los Angeles, down into the middle of the mix, and we stood a slight chance, and I mean slight, of getting the district attorney to prosecute this Pedi. So here is how it went down.

I went down to the guts of San Diego, oh I know; everybody thinks that San Diego is such a beautiful city to live in; what they don't know is that there are several streets of homeless people, crazy people, drug addicts, people in deep emotional pain, and prostitutes. I sought out my sister and found her walking the streets. I communicated to her what needed to be done, and I pleaded with her to get into my car. I committed to taking her shopping for new clothes that she could wear to the district attorney's office, cutting her hair, and even popping a few highlights in here and there. Do not forget that I still have that trusted cosmetology license in my back pocket. She reluctantly agreed.

Hopeful and believing that quite possibly the district attorney would not be able to detect all her shaking and sweating from the lack of drugs running through her system, a pair of white Levi's, and a white and pink blouse and white tennis shoes, and few snips of the scissors later, we headed northbound up to LA with my husband chauffeuring us. He was not thrilled, yet he still obliged.

We arrived early. Our appointment was at 10 a.m. With much anticipation, my husband, my sister, and I nervously sat in the waiting room. It had been a full day that Kathy had not had any drugs in her system, and yet she was able to function normally, or so I thought. The district attorney had read my accusations, so she was not as concerned about interviewing me because she knew where I stood. She was more concerned with interviewing Kathy to see if she could align with my truth.

A tall, lean middle-aged woman stepped into the waiting room with a very compassionate smile and said, "Which one of you is Kathy?"

My sister, very anxiously awaiting the interview, stood up and said, "I am."

The woman escorted her back into her office. At that point, I realized, *Whoa…we are here for Kathy and not me.*

My husband and I sat anxiously awaiting some sort of results, questioning if I would be able to withstand the pressure of the interview. Would I be able to get Kathy home quick enough? In my knower, I knew that it was going to set her off, and we were a long way from home. I did not want to lose her to the streets of Los Angeles and must go find her. After all, she was all dressed up compared to normal. We chit-chatted nervously. This waiting period seemed never-ending. It was either going to fly or not going to fly. Everything hinged on Kathy's interview. I was praying, asking God if He could please just intercede. *Can You please help the district attorney not see her for just another drug addict but one of the Pedi's victims?* Tormented.

About forty-five minutes later, the same lean kind-eyed woman opened the door, and my sister exited. As my sister went to sit down, the woman looked at me and said, "Can we talk? You're Cynthia, right?"

I said, "Yes, I am."

Gesturing toward the room behind her, she said, "We need to talk." My heart hit my stomach in dread just in the tone of her voice. As I entered her office, she asked me to have a seat.

She began by saying, "While I am not discrediting anything that this man did to you or your sister, and I believe you, and I believe your sister, we cannot proceed forth with this case."

Even though I knew the reason why, I still asked, "Why not?"

She explained to me that it was apparent to her that just getting my sister up there to LA was quite the task. It was too much of a risk versus the dollar amount that it would cost to *try* the case. She was certain that the possibility would be slim to none of a chance that Kathy would even be able to be found when push came to shove on the day of the trial. Disappointment.

She explained to me that Los Angeles County had tried a few *huge cases, you know the ones I mentioned earlier,* which had cost the county thousands of dollars, and that I was just a small fish in the big sea. That is how it was explained to me. She did, however, explain to me that if the district attorney's office caught wind of even one victim or even a hint of one child coming forth with allegations against this *Named Pedi,* I wouldn't have to be contacting her but that she would be contacting me as a witness.

I could tell that the woman was saddened for me and sickened that I did not have any other witnesses. She did add that if I were to be able to quickly find (with the one-year time constraint of the current California repressed memory law) other witnesses, I should have my attorney contact their office. As for my sister being a witness, they were not willing to take the gamble. Bummer.

I walked out of that office feeling very distraught and sick to my stomach, uncertain of what I should tell my sister. I knew lying to her was not the right thing, but was telling her the truth the right thing? After all, in my mind, I had it all figured out that if I could just keep her in my possession this time and get her into some sort of a program, everything was all going to work out. She was starting to shake and do the mouth-twitching thing that most all addicts do when in *need of a fix,* and I knew that my time with her was short. Not to mention that I had to explain to her what the district attorney had disclosed to me. I knew that she was going to run. I just did not know how bad it was going to get.

Three hours too long of a drive home by way of downtown San Diego. My sister understood explicitly that she was not going to make a good witness. Much to my surprise, because of where she was at in her life, she was relieved. Kathy did not quite understand that there was not going to be a criminal trial because of her lack of being a good witness, and I did not elaborate upon it either. Silence is *sometimes golden* when it comes to not disappointing your sister.

After getting through bumper-to-bumper California traffic, I relented to drop Kathy off on the streets that late afternoon with her freshly pumped up ego in her new pristine white Levi's. As I drove home, I was very solemn yet tearful. My husband barely said a word, which was not unusual for him. In the back of my pocket, I still had an ace. I made my mind up that day that I was going to use it. There was a suggestion from my attorney that she thought I could for sure go after him in a civil case. Just days before my appointment with the district attorney's office, we had gotten an approval to remove the John Doe name in our court filings and replace it with the Pedi's *real legal name.* This was a huge victory for both myself and my attorney. Onward Christian soldier.

The following morning, I placed a call to my attorney, and to no surprise of mine, she had already heard from the district attorney. It was not going to be possible. It just would not work. Civil suit it was—anything to draw attention to the Pedi's name.

I did not feel angry at my sister because she was an addict, but I did feel disappointed in the system. That they could not just take *my word* for what had happened to me but that I had to have a corroborating witness for it to be true. This was my truth. Why couldn't they just take me at my word? After all, I was an upstanding citizen in the community.

She did, however, give me a glimmer of hope and encouraged me that she felt that we could try and expose him civilly. And for that, I thought that at least I did not expose this already opened wound to the world for no reason. I desperately wanted to stop him from hurting others. And that was my only reason for the civil suit. Period.

The fire that seemed to ignite me and give me confidence and courage to proceed with this civil suit was the fact that when the Pedi was molesting me as a young child, my young body was still wounded from being burned. It sickened me to think of the depravity of the kind of person who would get enjoyment from a burned child's torment. Who in their right mind would sexually molest a child?

I began to analyze in my mind that he had picked my mother because she had two little toe-headed daughters and a toe-headed son. I had already endured being a victim through all the burns and the scaring, so I was emotionally weak. Ideal prey. I was fatherless, and I knew the emotions of abandonment at five years old. So here I was, desperate to be loved, *all battered up* in every area of my being. It looked like someone was going to love me. Walking through those emotions made me terrified for another little girl to have to go through. What choice did I have? I had to proceed civilly, even at the expense of completely losing my younger sister's companionship for good. Oddly enough, as much emotional pain as I was in, civil suit, here we come.

Switzerland

My relationship with my husband was emotionally hanging on by a thread. There was never talk of divorce or separation or anything of that magnitude, but the distance was becoming wider and wider and wider. Once it was clear to my husband that I was proceeding forth with a civil suit, understandably, he became very nervous and scared of what the public persona would perceive of our family. After all, he held a good position at the local power company, and he was afraid of being ousted, made fun of, mocked, you know all the above. At no point did he ever encourage me to explain things or ask questions unless I first volunteered the information. It really was not his battle to fight. His battle was to keep his marriage together as it seemed to be slowly slipping away.

Each day, as I was battling what felt like an endless encounter seemingly alone, I became more and more agitated with my husband. At the same time, he was silently getting more and more frustrated himself about our slipping lifestyle charade.

The mounting late notices appearing on our front door from the various utility companies did not help the thick emotions. Both of us could read each other quite well, but instead of confronting our impounding fears, we played a sick dance all the time. Tension was building. What happens when tension is mounting? It eventually blows.

One particular day when I did not receive the cheerleading affects that I was so desperately waiting to hear, I finally exploded, telling him exactly how his actions were making me feel. I explained to him that I didn't care if I had to go sell my house and go live in an apartment or voluntarily repo my car, that there was no material thing that was worth stopping me from exposing this Pedi. If he did not get on board, then he could find the front door. I assured him that I did love him, but for the first time in my life, I was learning to love myself more.

Sadly, there was not a whole lot of change after that argument to tell you the truth. I wish there had been, but there was not. That was just his way, his personality. He is very balanced, neutral. Switzerland. *On the inside, I knew that he wanted me to find peace; he was just scared of the process.*

After standing up to my husband that day, I continued my journey, as hard as it was. I felt God strongly encouraging me, whereas my husband was not. If it were not for God, then I would not have the small shred of sanity left that I was holding on to. I became vulnerable to my husband that day. A side of me that was not often seen.

I am kind, giving, and generous, but vulnerability was not on the description page for Cindy. That day, the Spirit of God got ahold of me right in front of my husband. I think it was about the lowest low I had gotten to in my plight to stop this Pedi. Quite possibly the position that God wanted me in. I explained to him that day that I would rather obey God than man, and I reaffirmed to him that he knew my stance in the Lord. I understood my husband ignoring me. This had become his typical behavior at that time. He was trying to get me to pull back and not go forth. He thought that by ignoring me and not talking to me about what it was that I was going through, it would cause me to collapse in my decision about suing this man. Yes, at this point, I was suing my Pedi. That is what a civil suit equates to. Monetary bribery...basically.

If I could have exposed him in a different way than a civil suit, I would have chosen it. I explained to him that, did I wish that the Pedi would get some help, change, and become a better person? Yes. But from all the research that I had done on Pedis, this was not going to just happen. I needed to do what I felt I was *called* to do, which was to expose him for who he *really was* behind his facade and what he had done to me. I reiterated how sorry I was that all this mess was trying to ruin our marriage.

Silence hit our home hard like a storm that day, even more than I had previously experienced. I knew that love would prevail because that is what the Word of God says. I believe the Word of God. Love always wins, and I was depending on that this time because I dearly and deeply loved my husband to a depth that most people never really get to experience. O the love of another human being.

Awkward Carriage Ride

Prior to remembering the molestations, my other sister, the Pedi's daughter, had a very large and elaborate wedding that I was struggling to be involved in because I knew that the Pedi would be there. While I had not remembered him molesting me at this time, I did, however, remember that he had molested my sister, and I did not want to be around him. He scared me. My daughter loved her aunt. She almost idealized her and kind of wanted to be like her. Driven, goal-oriented, outspoken, something that my daughter was not. She was more inclined to weigh her words just like her daddy.

I was chosen to be a bridesmaid; you see, being a maid of honor included much more responsibility, planning, and being involved in the planning. While I was offended that I was not chosen as a maid of honor, I was not surprised. But my daughter was surprised and offended greatly, and I watched her slightly pull away from her aunt. It was the beginning to a slow end.

One of the responsibilities that we were asked to help with was in the meal preparation. I could not believe that my sister had the nerve to ask me to help skin chicken breasts, possibly as many as three hundred of them and that this chicken skinning was going to be held at the Pedi's house.

In a strange way, I thought it was a test that my sister was putting me through. Like a test of how much I really loved her. *You say that you are my sister, well…this is what you need to do for me.*

We show up to skin the chicken breast the night before the wedding, my husband, my emotional cheerleader of a daughter, myself, and the Pedi's second wife. She seemed like a nice lady. Odd.

Unbeknownst the Pedi was there also. For the life of me, I did not think that he would be there. When I said I would skin the chicken breasts, I automatically assumed he would not have the nerve to be hanging around. Weird. But then again, why wouldn't he be?

No sooner did we all start skinning the chicken as he sat in the other room, he began throwing questions at me. He asked the most peculiar questions as if he was trying to get at something. He asked about my mother and how she was doing in a very sarcastic tone. He asked about my baby brother and how he was coming along in his life. He even had the nerve to ask about Kathy. But he never asked how I was doing. He was on a *fishing expedition,* though I did not realize it at the time, nor did he realize at that time that I did not remember that he had molested me. With each question and the sound of his voice, I became more filled with an overwhelming fear and anxiety. I kept telling myself that I was doing this for my baby sister and not for him. We could not peel the skin off those chicken breasts fast enough.

I kept looking over at my husband with eyes that said, "Get me out of here."

He did not skin one chicken breast; after all, was that not beneath him? Looking back, I can see that he thought he had me right where he wanted me, not realizing that I did not remember at this point what horrors he had done to me as a child.

We returned to our hotel, which we as a family still jokingly refer to as the *five-dollar hotel.* Everything you needed would be an additional five dollars. You need a roll-away bed; that will be five dollars. You need a plunger, five dollars. "Periwinkle Purple Hotel, five dollars please" was laughed about for days to come. God knew that we were desperate for some sense of joy and humor in all this dysfunctional sickness. Oh, the lengths that a sister will go out of love for her own sister.

The following morning in preparation for the wedding, something shifted in me. Something did not feel right. I felt extremely anxious, and I kept having panic attack after panic attack for like four hours, but I did not know that was what they were called at the time. That did not stop them from coming like a crashing wave. I put on my hideous dress. I entered the room full of girls and the dress that was picked out for me, which I later turned into an even more horrendous pillow covering and eventually threw away. It was very bothersome to me. The fit of the dress was way too sexual for my comfort. Remember I was the prude in the family. While others walked around the room in their undergarments with no conviction, I spotted another female relative in the room. While I had not recovered my memories yet, the thought had crossed my mind, *I wonder if he molested her like he did my sister Kathy.* After all, she was a known *pole dancer* and appeared to be proud of it as she attempted to alter the way in which she wore the dress. She had pushed both shoulders down to make it more seductive for others to view, trying to make it as suggestive as possible. My poor daughter sat in the room watching all this drama taking place.

There ended up being a verbal and almost physical fight between my baby sister, the one getting married, and her half-sister screaming and fighting and name-calling to the max because the bride specifically stated repeatedly that "This is my day and not yours." "All of the spotlight should be on me, so have some respect." The wedding could not start soon enough. The pole dancer never did pull those dress shoulders back up. The show must go on. Bridezilla.

I felt like I was in a trance. Something was happening on the inside of me, and I did not even realize it. The blindfold was slipping, and I did not even know it. It was as if I were an observer in my own body. You know how things always happen for a reason. While we may not be able to explain it as it is happening, we can, however, look back on it and say, "Oh wow, that is why that happened." Well, once the wedding was over, the charade of a reception began, and the joke of my broken family started in.

The strangest thing was that there were like fifty little preteen girls, you know a Pedi's profile, all running around setting up these reception tables. One having napkins, one having silverware. You see, the Pedi was married to the *director of the Simi Valley Girl Scouts*. It was explained to me that all these little girls were working toward earning a hospitality badge. Convenient. It was the eeriest, most obscure reception as the little girls began serving the plates to people with those chicken breasts that my daughter and I had skinned the night before.

As soon as the ceremony ended, within minutes, I went and changed out of that dress. I found myself trying to hide my body, and I could not figure out what was going on. I felt like the Pedi was raping me with his eyes as I wore that dress. I could not get out of that dress off fast enough and change into the oversized T-shirt that I had packed. Safer.

As soon as the parade of the sitting portion of the reception was completed, it was announced that there would be a chariot ride at the pleasure of the bride and groom, and they wanted everyone to enjoy a tour.

For some bizarre reason, I sickly encouraged my daughter to go for a ride on this horse and buggy with the Pedi and his granddaughter from the topless dancer. It was almost like someone else had taken over and was bullying her into doing this bizarre act. She was adamant that she did not want to take a ride, but I pressured her, assuring her that it was going to happen. She looked at me like, *Really? What the heck is going on?* she silently asked with her eyes as she timidly boarded the chariot. She sat on one side, and the Pedi sat opposite her with his three-year-old granddaughter, the flower girl from the ceremony snuggled up next to him. Awkward dysfunction. He stared frozen and awkwardly at her, and she returned the stare in just as much awkwardness. It was a silent, never-ending loop around the beautifully manicured gardens. One time around was enough for my daughter, and she eagerly exited that chariot.

Little did we know that God, in His infinite timing, was using this whole wedding experience to pry open these long-lost memories out of their hiding place and bring them up to the surface to where they ultimately belonged.

I began feeling stranger and stranger and had no clue what was really going on within me. Why had I been so adamant that my daughter was to ride in this chariot with this Pedi? I felt furious and vile and exposed. I could not seem to get out of this place quick enough without offending my baby sister.

Kathy had already caused offense by not showing up to the wedding. Kathy, who was currently in a sober living twelve-step home, was originally asked to play the guitar and sing for the wedding, and she excitingly accepted the privilege. That was until the bomb was dropped that the Pedi put on the wedding invitation that he would be giving this bride away. Pleasure instantly snuffed out.

We always protected my baby sister from the truth of her father growing up. She did not know all that her father had done to Kathy until she was an adult. We played into what my baby sister *became as an adult* with the way we catered to her.

My relationship with my daughter after the wedding, oddly enough, seemed to get closer. My daughter could see what an idiot this Pedi was. Riding on the chariot that day, I believe she saw what a charade my whole childhood had been. It was just a paradigm of the truth that I was still living in.

No More Blindfolds

Within weeks of this wedding, the blindfold was removed. Unfortunately, it was not removed slowly. It was one very painful dream at a time. I am a very smart woman. I was smart enough, as I said earlier, to document these dreams, and so the Ferris wheel began. I would have the second dream and then a third, fourth, fifth, and a sixth dream. These dreams were the basis of my claim against the Pedi. These dreams would either free me or be the death of me. In the end, these dreams brought me freedom from fear, phobias, and frights.

Nightlights became my friend. Once these dreams began rearing their ugly head, innocently, I began buying nightlights. I know I should have been paying my bills instead. There was a nightlight in the bathroom. A nightlight in the kitchen. I put a nightlight in the upstairs hall. It was a known fact not to dare shut them off. I did not really realize what I was doing at the time, nor did I really care; I just knew that I felt safety in having these nightlights on.

Each time that the Pedi would molest me, he would turn that bathroom light near my bedroom off. I can only guess it was to keep my mom from waking up, or if she did wake up, she would stumble in the dark hallways. When that light went off, as I lay awake, I knew that he was coming into my room. So there was a psychological aspect to these nightlights being on. No more molesters. It was my way of saying that this was sacred ground.

There was a devil out there, like a roaring lion who seeks to devour and destroy. He was alive and kicking, trying his best to scare me off and to hang onto the territory that he had already claimed when I was a child. This was a physical claiming of this territory away from the devil and into God's hands. No more darkness. I folded my blindfold neatly, tucking it away, and vowed to never wear it again, no matter the cost, in any area of my life. No longer deceived.

Pedophilia has many parts to it. There is no set person that becomes a Pedi. They come in all different molds. The one common denominator is that they all scout out their victims. They do their homework. They plot, manipulate, scheme, and plan. They get good at the task at hand.

My Pedi had far too much experience, and I was becoming quickly aware of the fact that I probably was not his first victim with each memory.

While I felt that it was necessary to go forth with this civil suit so that I could work out my own freedom and find the stolen liberty missing from my soul, I had an even deeper compulsion driving me, and that was to stop him from molesting other little girls. As I wrote at the very beginning of this book, when he called me on the phone, what kept resonating through me was his sarcastic and self-righteous attitude and tone. With that attitude, my inner child knew that he was still unchanged. What was I to do? What choice did I have? *Do I turn a blind eye?* God forbid—I had already put my blindfold up.

"Flee fornication. Every sin that a man doeth is without the body; but he that committeth fornication sinneth against his own body" (1 Corinthians 6:18).

For I knew that I was bought with a price and that I served a living God. God wanted me to be strong. God knew that I could do this assignment. Yes, that is what it was, an assignment from God. I was to stand up for myself. I could do it. I would do it. I will do it.

Just knowing that you are called to stand up for a specific situation is not enough. You also must wait for the anointing of God before you approach the situation head-on. I chose to stand on the foundation of the Word of God and to receive His word that He had spoken to me to move forward. No matter where it landed me. I thank God for this new season, this newfound hope that this Pedi would be exposed. I had nothing to hide. There were no skeletons in my closet, nor were there going to be *any more skeleton winters*. So off to the attorney's office I marched.

Lacking Viable Victims

I now had the task of explaining in multiple conversations to my husband, my kids, my siblings, and my mother that we didn't have what the DA considered to be a strong enough material case for an indictment but that we would be moving forward with a civil case against the Pedi.

My attorney prepared all the legal documentation that was necessary to have the Pedi served with the civil suit. Finding him and getting him to receive service was a task in and of itself. According to my attorney's belief, it appeared as if he was dodging service. Typical behavior of a Pedi.

Eventually, we did have him served. About a month later, my attorney contacted me to let me know that he had retained an attorney and that a response would soon be following. The response was *one big fat denial* of all facts. Typical behavior. Mind you, the previous phone call of admission was a great blessing to me in this time. What I had was the truth to fall back on, and *that never fails you because it never changes.*

I knew that I was in for quite a Lewis and Clark expedition. Long journey ahead. I was not sure every day if I could go through it. Some days I was stronger than others. We were no longer dealing with just the Pedi; his attorney was now a screen that he could hide behind, as was probably because all Pedis are cowards. One bonus to this screen was that he agreed to accept service for his client from here on out. At least we would not have to work for weeks the next time he needed serving. Under the jurisdiction of the same judge who originally reviewed the allegations, we were able to go forth and have the Pedi served with the civil lawsuit and make our claims in our filed complaint of childhood sexual abuse, intentional infliction of emotional distress, negligent infliction of emotional distress, assault, and sexual battery and damages. Case number EC015467, Superior Court of the state of California, for the county of Los Angeles, Northern Central District/Burbank.

While this was not where the Pedi lived at the time, it was the county in which the assaults took place when I was a child. This was a huge victory as this case number was assigned a name. Along with it was *the order from* the *court* allowing the defendant John Doe to be named. Finally.

You see, there are a lot of steps that you must go through before you can *name a defendant in a civil suit.* We had just jumped through the final hoop to attach a *name to a case,* and we were finally able to get it filed in the court system.

Huge victory. This milestone took us close to a year to complete.

During the same time period, my attorney was waiting for all the responses to return back from the different doctors that I had seen throughout the years. While we were under time constraints regarding the one-year statute of limitations for negligent sexual abuse cases in Los Angeles County, my attorney had gone ahead and sent out anything that she thought might be subpoenaed preemptively so that we would have all of our ducks in a row.

My attorney contacted me and said that we needed to meet and asked when I could come in. I had racked up a fairly large bill. The ten-thousand-dollar retainer fee had all but been used up, and I had twice that that I now owed.

I had a hunch what the meeting might be about. I showed up to my attorney's office a few days later. She very graciously brought me into the big old not-so-scary-any-longer conference room. She sat me down and offered me some coffee, tea, or water. She explained to me that the law firm that she worked for took a vote and stated that they could no longer financially carry my case. It was really getting to be a stretch out of the realm of her expertise. Copywrite infringement vs. repressed memory cases. Big difference.

As I sat there, I knew that she was not going to leave me hanging. That was not her personality. She explained to me that she had reached out to her contacts and that she had found a local attorney that was known for going after these "creeps" who was willing to take on my case and see it to the end. While I felt somewhat defeated, I also felt hopeful that these newfound attorneys could use their plethora of knowledge to help me as we neared our assigned civil court date.

As I walked out of my attorney's office for the last time with a large oversized box full of copies of any and everything making up my case, it surprised me that she had the foreknowledge of the fact that I would accept these new attorneys because she copied everything in advance and had it all ready for me to walk out of the office with. I thanked her, and we both cried, and she encouraged me not to give up.

We may think that we have our way all mapped out, but God always has a better plan. Hopeful. I was feeling inspired that these new attorneys could get me to trial. For them to have already reviewed my case and found it to be one that they wanted to take on showed me that this was going to be victorious.

Two Little Bulldogs

An older gentleman in his late fifties and a younger in his early forties very kindly escorted me into their conference room. Just blocks away from my old attorney. My first reaction to the two *men* was I sure hope that I do not have to start fresh in my descriptions of the violations. That was not going to happen.

One reason that I was able to open up to my first attorney was that she was a female. But now, I had been handed these two males. I really was not sure if I had what it would take to do this. Men and I were not getting along very well at this point in my life. I saw them as the enemy. Understandably.

I had a seat, and right away, the older gentleman said, "We are going to get this bad man. I read your case, and we are going to shut him down." Hmmm, maybe he will work.

He continued, "What he did to you was insane and irreprehensible. We are going to get to the bottom of this one way or the other."

The younger one chimed in, shaking his head, saying, "I have tried several cases in my career and won, and I have no doubt that we can win this one too." The younger man continued by explaining that "We are aware that you want to go to trial." They knew that my goal was, as conveyed to him by my first attorney, to expose this man for who he really was. He wanted me to be aware that just by filing case number EC015467, it was already in the public arena. It was public knowledge. I did not quite get that day what they were expressing at the time.

What I did understand was that in order for them to proceed, I was going to have to scrape, beg, and borrow to come up with an additional five-thousand-dollar retainer fee.

I left that office that day encouraged that I was going to be able to proceed forth, and yet I was very concerned as to where I was going to come up with the extra five grand. God took me *to it,* and God would see me *through it.*

It had been explained to me that just the process to get into the courtroom with the jurors and the court reporter and to pay for the *use* of the courtroom would cost me a minimum of twenty thousand dollars out of pocket and upfront. Wow. Reality. I thought to myself, *This is just not fair.* I had gotten to the point where I just could not work *even if I tried.* I did not miss the office game, but I sure missed the income, and I needed it *desperately* just about now.

I resorted to going to my local loan office and taking out a personal loan so that I could put the down payment retainer fee to secure these two lawyers. My mother, of all people, loaned me the other half of the retainer fee. I did not want to take a dime from her, but she practically insisted. She knew that I was good for paying her back because I had always paid my debts. I had never borrowed anything, nothing from her. She had taught me well. There is always a *first* when you are in a desperate situation. I felt like such a hypocrite. I was a hypocrite. I could not stand being in the presence of my mom at this point, and yet I was taking money from her. Money that I was not sure as to when I could ever pay back. That is a definition of a hypocrite.

My next appointment with my new attorney's office was a little overwhelming for me. Unbeknownst to me, these bulldog attorneys never intended on going to trial. Looking back, I can now see the subtle comments that I did not notice at the time that hinted at this.

Instead, they were bulldog negotiators in civil suits. They were good at throwing around large dollar amounts in exchange for settling out of court. They had been in contact with the defendant's attorney and had received a dollar amount quote that the defendant was willing to pay in order to save face in a trial. I wanted to proceed with the trial. They honored my wishes for the time being.

As a next step, my attorneys asked me to undergo a psych evaluation in which I would be assessed by a psychiatrist who worked in the field of sexual molestations to victims and also worked hand in hand with the court system. I had not been all that impressed with any of the other doctors that I was going to anyway. I felt like I was just another co-pay just walking in the door. I reluctantly agreed.

They explained that they had received all of my past medical documentation and that what they were looking for was that I had never mentioned in any of my sessions of being molested by anyone prior to my date of first dream or memory. They confirmed that the records had already been established by my tellings.

Dr. Beatle Haircut

Driving my truck twice as far to meet this new recommended psychiatrist, I walked in, and he had this Beatle haircut and a leather couch that looked to be at least twenty years old, a golden-brown rust in color wrinkled leather-like look. He asked me to have a seat. I looked to see what part of the couch was the plumpest to sit on. This was the real deal. People really had lain down on this couch like on TV.

He introduced himself to me with a handshake, which with my experience, not a lot of doctors were doing these days. He said, "This first session is going to be a lot of questions and answers. Do you think you can do that?"

I said, "I will do the best that I can." This doctor seemed different than anyone that I had ever gone to.

He explained that "This may be more like an hour and a half session." He noticeably did not sit through the session staring at his watch like doctors in the past had done with me.

He explained to me that he was not on my insurance company's list of preferred providers. Stop sign. Right away, I thought, *Oh, we have a problem here*. But he assured me that this was not going to be a problem. That he was going to file *for an exclusion*. That this was necessary for me to have him as my professional medical advisor.

I thought, *Okay*. "Are you sure?" I asked him.

He said, "Don't worry about it. I am more concerned about your mental health, and I have it approved."

Right away, once the financial side of things was resolved, he started in on the interrogation. Who I was, how I had gotten to where I was at, but most of all, he got down to the nitty-gritty of how I was feeling. With all this civil case and back pocket possibilities of a criminal trial going on, nobody really wanted to know how I was *feeling.*

I was very honest with him, and I said, "I am *depressed and worried,* and I feel like I am *a nervous wreck* most of the time."

He assured me that *if* we went to trial, notice I said the word *if,* he would be there by my side. From what he had read in the legal documents, he assured me that *he believed me* and that I was strong-willed enough emotionally to get through to the end.

Here is the thing, when you are in the middle of the *whirlwind of repressed memory,* you do not really think about other people's grand finale or, for that manner, other people's needs.

While yes, the doctor was a licensed psychiatrist, and he was good at his work because he had passion as well as compassion, his end result was that he worked to get paid. He continued interviewing and counseling for an almost double session. It was not something that he could get all answered or resolved in that short of time. He needed to get through the interviewing process. Through the events of being molested in order to get to the now, the current day living that I was in. After all, he was a psychiatrist, and he wanted to make sure that I was properly medicated if that was what I needed so that when I would proceed forth with any further dealings in this court case, I was not going to go jump off a bridge or something, and he told me as much. He assured me that he was there to help me and that he was on my side until the end.

In conjunction with the Zoloft that I was taking for depression, he wrote me two additional prescriptions. One for anxiety attacks and a dissolvable pill for panic attacks. This was the first time that it was being explained to me that I was experiencing major *anxiety.* It had always just been explained to me that it was just depression. This was the first time that I understood the difference between *anxiety attacks and panic attacks.*

Anxiety attacks are like...*I can't do it; I can't do it; well, maybe I can do it; I think I can do it*, and as the anxiety lifts, you look back, and *you did it.* They usually last about fifteen to twenty minutes, is how it was explained to me, sometimes less and sometimes more, and that it was always linked to the fear of the unknown. The *what ifs*, the *what abouts*, or the *how comes*.

Panic attacks, on the other hand, there was really no negotiating with. They stop you dead in your tracks. While the same fear is behind a panic attack, it comes on like a violent crashing earthquake, and you cannot do much of anything. Zero functioning capability. Complete debilitation.

Wow. This doctor, though he thought that he was extracting information from me, had given me more new information than anyone before. I was categorizing every word that he said. In the last part of the session, he did something for me that no one had done; he began to validate my pain.

While I do not like to claim it as my own pain, it was my pain. He explained to me that I had been carrying that pain around with me everywhere that I went and that it had affected every relationship that I had had in my entire life. He encouraged me that it was time to drop off the pain and put it back where it belonged.

In addition, he told me that he *believed me on many different levels.* Such a small thing that meant so much.

That day he went through every one of the document molestations that were on file, and he had me walk through all six of them as he followed along with the incident report in his hand. When we got through it all, he then explained to me that he absolutely, 100 percent, believed everything that I was telling him.

Not only did he believe that I believed it, but he believed that it really *did happen* to me. He said that "If you have me as your doctor, I would like to help you."

I said, "I have one question for you." And I proceeded to tell him that my mom had a psychologist as a third husband and that "I don't want any *fake do-it-to-get-paid doctor* trying to help me." So I needed to know what propelled him to become a psychiatrist.

He very humbly explained to me that both his mother and brother were mentally ill. One of them had committed suicide. He had made a covenant with himself that when he got educated, he would help as many people as possible. Compassion expressed.

I left the office that day with a newfound religion. That God is in the work of the psychiatrist. He would send anything in my path to help me. I agreed to a total of ten sessions a month, as was recommended. Three sessions one week and two sessions the next. Gasoline increase.

Lil Cindy's Cookie Castle

Unable to work in real estate, I sat down one day and tried to figure out what it was that I could do to make some sort of a contributing income to our family. Something where I did not have to have a dress code like in the fast-paced real estate industry. I had always loved to bake. In high school, I dreamed of becoming a home economics teacher; that is before life had its way. I had taken an experimental cooking class when I was in eleventh grade, and out of it, I had created several different recipes. Cookies, brownies, and candies: that was my forte.

While I had lost interest in many things, softball teams, softball friends, or just friends in general, I had not lost my love for baking. I got a natural high from baking, a thrill, if you will.

Not even realizing it, when the anxiety came upon me, baking was a way that I managed the anxiety. For me, anxiety is a bunch of balled-up neurotic energy trying to find its way out of the body. By baking, I was giving it a route to escape. I was trying to take this negative and turn it into a positive.

I have always been a faith finder, for the most part. I knew going through all these repressed memories that there had to be something *good that God wanted to come out of it.* That day, thinking about what I could do to supplement our household income, I came up with the idea of starting a cookie business.

I got my journals out, as I often did, and I started creating a business all on paper. I named it Lil Cindy's Cookie Castle. That day I named every cookie that I would want to bake. Each cookie had a unique title. There was Knights in Chocolate, which was a chocolate cookie with a chocolate chip. "Yum," said my daughter. There was Queen's White Delight, which was an oatmeal base with an added white chocolate chip, etc. My favorite was Princess Pecan

Peanut, an excellently designed peanut butter cookie; one of the best anyone has ever baked if you ask me. Each with its own distinctive name. I did all of this in just a few hours' time. Amazingly fun.

My husband came home from work that day only to hear about my found new expedition. His first thought was, *How can we possibly afford this?* I assured him that it would be one step at a time. He had baked with me in bulk in our past years together and had enjoyed the spoils. He knew that I could make one mean German chocolate-covered brownie. So he was not hard to convince. He said with a shrug, "Let's try it." Wow, I was so elated that something was on the horizon after having sat around for a year now, going through this heap of vomit of court filings.

Even if I did not make any profit at selling these cookies, then at least I would have an outlet that would help me *feel important.* One of the key things that I had lost was a sense of value. Amid all that was going on around me week by week, I began putting into motion the beginnings of a small in-house bakery. I bought my convection ovens from an old closed bakery. Slowly, as I could afford it, I bought my sheet pans, my product tables, my labels, product baggies, and my sealing plastic/product heat machine. I even had T-shirts designed and printed. I found the money by faith to put all of this together. It gave me a sense of purpose and a way to get my mind off dwelling on all *this other legal court stuff.*

New Job Possibilities

Around this time, my husband began bringing home little rolled-up pieces of fax paper that he had shoved in his briefcase. When he would arrive home, he would unroll them, revealing to me job offers that he had been receiving on a daily basis from around the country. In my recent journals, I could remember discussing with God how it was possibly time for me to get out of this big city. How it would not displease me at all to get away from all the concrete and asphalt, not to mention all the crowds in the most basic places like the grocery store. The two were starting to line up like...Hmmm? Maybe it is time (down the road...soon...) for us to leave California and move on and out.

I asked God for a sign that night. I prayed and asked God if He could give my husband a monetary bonus. He had been traveling with the company he worked for, for the past three years. They had assigned him to a special software project, and it was just winding down and was almost completed. So I very boldly asked God for a specific dollar amount gratuity bonus *as a sign* from Him and a confirmation that soon we would be moving. I just did not know where that move would take us.

Over the next several months of us baking, when I least expected it, he would bring home another fax from yet another job offer that he had received. After about the third one, I confided in my daughter and asked her how she felt about the idea of moving. She was the only other kid we needed approval from since the boys were at an age where they were living their own lives. Much to my surprise, after all, she said sure she would not mind that at all, but where was I talking about?

One of the offers was in Texas, and that was out of the question. We did not want to move to New York. New Mexico either. My husband and I agreed, along with my daughter, that if, in fact, we were going to be moving, then we needed to all agree as to where it would be and that we needed to get this long-drawn-out court case under the blood. At this point, it was not just about me and being sexually molested, repressed or not; it was about keeping my family together. If it was something that we were going to do, then it had to be *three yeses.*

Good Bazooka Times

Traveling ten times a month back and forth to my new psychiatrist's office was a double-edged sword. It was an hour each way in my big 350 truck that I was still able to hang onto along with its huge payment and large gas bill. Getting emotional relief from this very talented and gifted doctor of mine was on the other side of the spectrum and well worth the travel as I popped my Bazooka bubblegum as my new daily fix to escort me along with my travels.

The weight gain was accelerating as I had found a liberty in pretty much eating whatever I wanted to for the first time in my life. I had always enjoyed my Bazooka bubblegum because it reminded me of my dad when I was a kid. I would rock back and forth on the couch in-between, stopping to pop some of my Dentyne and Bazooka gum in my mouth. Seems kind of silly but blowing those Bazooka bubbles was a way that I could expel some of the pent-up energy each time that I would attempt to blow a bubble even bigger and bigger. My husband would just shake his head at me.

I tried to explain the Bazooka addiction to my doctor, and he said, "What about it? What's wrong with it?" He said, "It sounds to me like we are on the brink of doing some inner child work." That was a journey in and of itself. One for a later date.

A large part of me was starting to feel healthier and healthier. This doctor really allowed me to see that it was okay for me to come out of the pain. He confirmed to me that it was PTSD but explained to me that due to my court case, he needed to add a new request to my plate. My attorneys had contacted him and said that they now needed me to undergo some IQ testing, which was going to add even more to my travels.

Lifelong Friend

While my husband was busy holding a job down, which I could not do at the time, my lifelong friend Joann took the requested journey with me for the intensive IQ testing that was taking place on the other end of Los Angeles, in the heart of San Fernando Valley, a good four hours from home. Amazingly, the very valley in which my molestations took place. That in and of itself made me a nervous wreck. So I employed the company of my lifelong friend to come alongside of me. I was afraid to drive in all the bumper-to-bumper traffic.

While my relationship with God was strong and ongoing, I had a bit of a bad taste in my mouth. You see, this IQ testing was being done by yet again another psychiatrist. Another male psychiatrist. Here goes that trust factor again. Thank goodness for my friend who did most of the driving and who did all the parking. Chuckle.

IQ testing is very interesting. While I did not quite understand all the timers that were being set with each segment of the testing, I later was able to determine that it was all part of it. While I am sure that each test has its own precise way, the testing that I underwent included shapes, objects, a lot of mathematical questions that needed answering in a timely fashion. What I did not know was that this doctor was hired for one reason, to determine how smart I was, how educated I was, and how employable *I was or was not* for future employment in a different profession.

Once all the testing was done, about four hours later, I did not realize that the doctor was going to bring me in his office right then and there to go over the results with me. The doctor explained to me that "It is not every day that I am asked to do testing on a genius." Yes, that is what he said. I looked up at him and said, "A genius?"

He said, "Yes. You tested out on a genius IQ level. There is nothing that if you *put your mind to it*, you could not do aside from possibly being a doctor." He continued, "Because your high school grades fall shy of a 3.9." I always wondered after the fact where he received the information about my high school grades.

It was an interesting day that day. One with an unforeseen outcome. The doctor was hired to do this testing on me so that the attorney handling my case could put *a dollar value* on my *future employment* possibilities. It was quite peculiar how they equate intelligence to employment earnings. All I thought as I walked out of the building was that I wanted to eat one of those cookies that we baked the day before. We had packed our lunch for this excursion because we were practically near broke *but for the grace of God*.

Parallel Trips

Within weeks of the IQ testing, I needed to make another trip up to the same area because it was time for me to take the dreaded deposition, which was required by both parties prior to trial. We still had our court date on the docket with all the intentions to proceed forth to a trial. My very faithful friend accompanied me again. Daunting.

I had spoken with my doctor on a few occasions regarding me being scared out of my gourd to have to sit across the table from the defendant, the Pedi. To be in that close of a proximity with him was terrifying. Vile. My doctor would tell me, "You know that little white pill I gave you for panic attacks? Wear something that you can put one or two of those in your pocket so that you can easily access them. Whatever you do...do not look at *him in the face*. These kinds of people, that's how they try and get you, *eye contact*." So I took his advice, kept it in the back of my mind, and kept telling myself that I could do this. I was becoming my own best cheerleader.

I counted down the days that my deposition was scheduled for. I contacted my friend to ensure she would be able to go with me on this journey. I was convinced that this newfound freedom that I was beginning to walk in was just the thing that I needed to take alongside me when that day came. I was beginning to *thrive again. It looked like the end of this nightmare might just be in sight.*

Baking my cookies five days a week was giving me a sense of worth and value again. I suffered from this feeling of worthlessness that if I did not work or bring money into the door, that low self-esteem factor would attack me. So having a little backup money gave me a false sense of worth. At this point, I would take any worth, whether it was false or not. Even if it had to mimic the truth. Not healthy yet.

D-Day

Wow. Another long ride, here we go. Up super early, coffee cup in hand, loaded into my big ol' 350 again, and we drove up into the city. Very close again to where I had been victimized. This trip literally gave me heart palpitations. Mimicking what I would think would be close to a heart attack. We got parked with thirty minutes to spare. While my friend encouraged me and assured me that she would go in the building with me, they would not allow her to accompany me into the deposition room. Oh, how I desperately just needed someone who was familiar to me to be there beside me. While my attorney was there, that just was not the same as a lifelong friend.

I felt frozen in my truck like I just could not get out. I knew that taking my deposition was all part of the getting to trial. Without this step, the next could not happen. My attorney informed me that he had been told that the Pedi would be in the room sitting across the table from me. Never did it cross my mind that he would be too chicken to show up. He had already postponed his own deposition with one excuse or another. My attorney explained to me that he was trying to get me to *depose first*. That way, it could give the defense lawyer an edge on how creditable of a witness I *would or would not make* on the stand. He was the one on the defense, and he did not know exactly what I was going to disclose. He did not want to reveal anything that I had not remembered and incriminate himself any further. So I bit the bullet and went ahead and did my deposition first. I did not have anything to hide; it was all out on the table. Exposed.

I was determined to get through this without having to use one of those white pills. While they did instantaneously calm me down, my doctor had told me that they were to be used in the case of an emergency only. Strong willpower again.

The rest of the time, we sat in the truck talking and praying and hoping for a good turnout. For weeks I had been praying that God would bind him from showing up. I knew the power of my God. In my heart, my hope was that I would not have to see his face. I really did not care what it took to stop him from coming. Possibly a debilitating case of diarrhea? I just trusted God that He would stop him. O the mighty power of prayer.

When I felt that I could not postpone any longer, I said, "Okay, it's time. I have to get in there." I looked at the clock, and knowing the walk to get into the appropriate area of the building, we left with five minutes to spare.

As we entered the building, we were greeted by a pleasant receptionist who was awaiting my arrival. Though according to my watch, I had three minutes left till my appointment time, she escorted me into a room that was filled with several different people. As I scanned the room, I noticed my lawyer, what I would assume was his lawyer, a court reporter, and another woman. The Pedi was nowhere to be found. His attorney stood up and identified himself and acted as if he was going to shake my hand. That was not happening. He was not rude, but he was not cordial either. I nodded my head, keeping politely my hands tucked tightly by my side, and identified myself to the court reporter.

It was ready, start, go. It appeared as if the court reporter was ready, and the Pedi had not yet entered the room. My attorney spoke up and inquired, "Is your client going to be here today?"

The opposing attorney responded, "No, he had other commitments, and he could not make it here today."

I took a deep breath. I felt relieved. I was having a never-ending anxiety attack after as I sat there in the chair.

Immediately the opposing attorney began by asking me my name, my birth date, and my place of residence. His tone said it all. He was extremely accusatory in the volume of his words. I just hung on to my bootstraps, tried not to appear nervous, looking him in the face as often as possible, answering his questions as directly and effectively as I could. I had been previously instructed by my attorney to answer "yes," "no," "I do not recall," or to explain what I did recall. So I followed my attorney's lead.

As we got into the deposition, possibly thirty minutes into it, I noticed that my direct, definitive, and precise answers were getting underneath the opposing attorneys' nerves. He did not like my answers. It appeared as if he was going to go through each sexual violation. After the first violation, he tried to get me to waver and back off the accusations. He tried to imply as if I quite possibly had wanted the violations to happen. Sicko.

He proceeded forth onto the second violation in question, and he did not ask near the details. One of his questions was, "I noticed that you keep saying that every time that he violated you, he had been drinking. What kind of beer did he drink?" His tone implied, *Oh, so you think you remember so much.*

I answered, "Coors," proceeding to add, "in a brown bottle with a long neck. Not like you see nowadays where it has a little bit of a shorter neck. He carried a six-pack or two home with him every night."

He proceeded forth by saying, "Well, how do you know that he was drunk with regards to this second incident?"

I said, "Because he drank every night. That is what he did. When he was married to my mom, he was an alcoholic." For some reason, this stunted him.

After that, he did not go into the other violations. He started asking erroneous questions. You could visibly see him processing. There was a shift in his posture. Instead of continuing his predetermined course of questioning agenda, he decided to start asking me about my past work experience and income. He began probing me why I could no longer work. He began accusing me of being a liar. He went from making subtle hints that, *After all, aren't you just making this all up?* to realizing, *Wow…this woman really did get molested by my client.*

All of a sudden, he brought the deposition to a halt. Some people would have gotten mouthy, wanting to talk back, argue back. But I went on the advice of my attorney to say yes, yes, and no, no.

Within a blink of an eye, the deposition was ended. No white pill for me. I was dismissed from the room. I had turned and looked at my attorney, and he said that he would be giving me a call later in the week. I walked out of that room, and my friend was sitting right where I had last seen her waiting on me. She quickly inquired, "Did he show up? Was he there? I never did see him."

I responded back, "Nope, the coward never did show up." We very elatedly and in a giggly fashion, almost like the joy of the Lord was all over us, walked out, got in our truck, and ate the lunch that we had packed. Mini pack on ice. We entered back onto the freeway with a cookie in hand, trying to beat the dreaded LA afternoon traffic. Home sweet home never sounded so good. I did it!

What I did not realize then, but I now know, was that my attorneys were in negotiations with the Pedi's attorney. The Pedi was not interested in going to trial, nor was I. But I felt that it was something that I had to do and needed to do for all those little girls out there.

Decisions, Decisions, Decisions

For the most part, I was starting to get a grasp on how much pain I really was in. My tough exterior that had worked so well for me for so many years was slightly beginning to soften. While the civil suit seemed to be stagnating in the legal mumbo jumbo, hurry up and wait, my middle son had gotten married and made me a grandma for the first time. I was forced to look at my life and try and determine, *How important was all of this anyway?* Bringing a life into this world was much more important than going on and on about my miserable past of a childhood. Decisions, decisions, decisions, what is a girl to do?

Baking was fun. We made a little bit of money. Sometimes we would make three hundred dollars a day, which seems like a lot when you subtract it from nothing.

My husband seemed to be getting on board in the realization that his wife was indeed suffering from PTSD. He had escorted me into my doctor's office, and the doctor took the time to explain to him the depths of what it was that I was suffering from. It was not until the doctor explained the correlation to the trauma a Vietnam veteran would suffer that I saw a light go off in my husband's eyes. He was finally able to understand. Up until that session, it was as if he questioned most everything that I was going through and experiencing. At one point, he even said to me, prior to this session, "This is not what I signed up for." I knew that he did not really mean it. He loved me. He was just really scared. He was afraid of losing everything that we had worked so hard for.

My daughter, on the other hand, though we had not determined if we were, in fact, going to move or remain in San Diego County, enjoyed the weekly visits to the library researching the different states that these proposed jobs were located in. One of the states that he was offered a position in was having a lot of difficulties with the new rules and regulations that were being handed down by the federal government regarding the power industry. So that state was quickly taken off the table. Another one of the states was far too cold for our San Diego blood, we thought. For now, we just held our peace and waited for another offer to come in. Faith in motion. What I knew for sure was that my daughter had agreed to make the move should the time come. That said a lot, as she was just finishing up her junior year of high school.

Pedophilia Uncovered

There was a certain small percentage of me that was struggling with ruining this man's family life, which included my baby sister. He had a second wife of many years and a ten-year-old daughter from this wife. One would say, "Why would God choose to give him two daughters?" but that is not for us to speculate.

Predators plot out methodically their prey. It is part of the high. They watch their victims, checking out their personality types. They scout out the family dynamics. It is a very sick person who becomes a Pedi. I believe that one is *not born a Pedi*, but you, instead, *become a Pedi* through a series of wrong, bad, and evil choices. Interestingly enough, a large percentage of Pedis have been beaten as children and or molested themselves. In my caretaking observations and findings through reading the Surgeon General's almanac on pedophilia, I had a sick heart of compassion for this perverted Pedi as he had boasted about being severely beaten as a child. He would use this information to insight fear upon us children, saying, "Don't think I'm not afraid to beat the hell out of you... I got the hell beat out of me as a kid," letting you know just how tough he was. He also used that to insight guilt so that you felt sorry for him. It was a way that he would weaken our emotions. Any time you are feeling sorry for someone, you become vulnerable. *The O Poor Me syndrome.*

Once the Pedi zeroes in on who their next victim is going to be, one of the first tactics that they initiate is to incite fear upon you. They must prime you, poking and prodding, all part of their sick dance. Placing little particles of mistrust between you and anyone that you love or rely on. Any person in authority. Anyone you would dare tell.

My Pedi already had it figured out from what I can assume were previous molestations of others as to how to play me and how to play my sister in a different way. Not to mention how to play my mom because that was an important obstacle in the way of his prize.

There is a difference between Pedis and sexual predators. A Pedi is a sexual predator, but a sexual predator is not always a Pedi. Pedis are most interested and often drawn to underdeveloped pre-adolescent children. Sexual predators, now that is a different cup of tea. They may have their preferences, but they will harm anybody. In my case, and as I have determined with this particular Pedi, he was weak because he wore his emotions on his sleeve. What he had was a daughter and a son from my mother that he loved and cared about in his own sick way. In the beginning, he would tell me how sorry he was after molesting and violating me. He would add *how sorry daddy was,* and *he would never do it again* with tearful promises.

As I began to mature and develop, it turned to an angry violence on to the next prize. Less like father and daughter and more like rapist and victim. It was as if the fact that I was maturing made him angry because he was sickly attracted to children, and I was beginning to develop. The thrill was no longer there for him.

So my Pedi may very well have been a combination of sexual predator slash Pedi. This new knowledge that I was gaining fueled me and propelled me, igniting my courage to do what I knew needed to be done.

Sometimes in life, particularly in my situation, part of the payoff for freedom is giving up those that *appear* closest to you. Those relationships, for me, really were a *stumbling block to being completely liberated and set free from the bondage that Satan clearly sat out to lock me up into.* So I carefully disconnected, giving up all claims to any role I held, caretaker, fixer, rescuer; you know all the basic twelve step stuff that they teach you. I set my sails toward righteousness, rightness, restoration, wholeness, and right thinking. All the things that had been robbed from me and that needed restoration.

Hoping and believing that in the end, God would set everything in the right order for His name's sake.

As I began to *rise up out of the ashes of my past,* God began to fuel me with thoughts that *I could do this* and that *I had a right to do this.* He gave me the strength to stand up for myself. To believe in myself. To love myself. Yes, I had lost my real estate career. Had I put my hope in the wrong area? Yes, I had. It was not about material possessions. It was not about the fancy house and the fine dining living. Even though that is what I had made it. I was beginning to realize that *it* was all just a cover-up. A cover-up created by me to keep me from getting to the bottom of all this ugliness I was feeling. All these things for a season mimicked the feeling of happiness, but once the blindfold was taken off, I was able to see the insignificance of all the material treasures. My clear pool waters. My fancy lifestyle. To none avail.

"For what shall it profit a man, if he shall gain the whole world, and lose his own soul? Or what shall a man give in exchange for his soul?" (Mark 8:36–37)

If all else fails for the Pedi, they could go into the line of being a PI. Of course, I am being sarcastic, but that is what happens to a victim trying to cope; they become very sarcastic.

The sick part about the Pedi is that they believe their own *lies.* They have told the same *deceptive lie over and over* of how that child needs them in their life or how that child can't live without them that before you know it, they believe what they are saying to be truth. One sick individual, if I do say so myself.

Unraveling those *lies* from the victim's life can take years. But it can be done. Even down to the small innuendos and illusions of sexual abuse, like standing on the top of the steps naked to try and discipline and intimidate a child with your blatant nakedness. A child is affected and will carry with them these shocking illusions and disparaging images. Definition of "innuendos": an allusive or oblique remark action or hint, typically a suggestive or disparaging one.

Recently, as of five years ago, I had a memory of the very first time that my Pedi molested me. It is interesting how God works. You know the first shall be last, and the last shall be first. It just came out of the blue; it did not come through the dream this time. I guess one would say that my mind felt safe enough to remember it without any fear of intimidation or accusations.

In this memory, the Pedi and my mother had just started dating when he felt he had the liberty to come and pick me up from elementary school and leave my older sister to ride the bus home. I remember the office staff coming into my classroom to gather me and walk me to the office where the Pedi was waiting for me. In the walk from the classroom to the office, the office attendant commented to me that "Oh, you are going to a doctor's appointment, aren't you?"

Doctor's appointment? Huh? Not that I was told. I will keep that to myself, I thought. As we entered the office, there was the Pedi sitting there. I had nothing to fear...yet. He had never harmed me. We got into his vehicle, and he acted as if he was doing me a favor picking me up from school so that I did not have to endure the long bus ride home. I remember asking him, "What about my sister Kathy?"

And his conniving ways began as he proceeded with, "You are the special one. That's why I came to get you." I was perfect inventory, coveted by him, already scared and ready for his sick indulgent ways.

He drove me to my house, and he had the key to get in. *Guess Mom trusts him.* He proceeded to give me a course in sexual education and all my body parts right there on my own living room couch. It was in this memory that God began to explain to me the depths of destruction that occur to a poor innocent child, all at the fleeting benefit of the Pedi. When God gave me this memory, He began to show me the detailed mental configuration that a Pedi goes through just to molest one victim. That it is not just a spontaneous act; it is a plotted-out plan where they are always looking for an escape route where they do not get caught. The reason I say this so clearly and so knowingly is that I never told my mom that I got picked up from school early because he said that "It is our little secret." The sad part was that I believed him. It is no secret any longer. Pedis are bad, bad people. And they do very wrong things to children.

I encourage you that if you are a victim, *it is time* for you to speak out. Get a support system in place. Justice will prevail in the end. Sometimes it looks like justice is not going to play out because of the Pedi's deliberate acts upon you, but I am here as proof that justice will play itself out.

Wholeness is possible. Remember that completion is a process; the process is a will to the completion of the journey in your life. God wants to heal all the way down within you and around you, and it is not always something that He can perform instantaneously. Allow Him the time that He requires. There is a time for everything. We all know that. We have read it in Ecclesiastes repeatedly. But when you are a victim, for some reason, the time to get angry and to deal with that anger on the inside of you can be a journey that can sometimes feel that the ugliness that you are carrying on the inside of you, and the anger and the darkness that you cry about at night are leading you down a wrong road.

However, I am here to tell you that *that anger needs to come out of you.* When it does, you will begin to experience life as you have always longed for. That anger is a block, and the block needs to be removed for your healing to be completed. You see, anger is a substitute for depression. And yet depression has been a shield for your sanity. Because the anger was so strong that it would have taken your life had it not turned to depression. Anger, when held onto and carried, causes you to sin.

For me, I had to let it go. I slowly allowed the anger to leave. God began to show me to turn my face no longer away from Him but to turn my face toward Him and that He could and would wipe my tears, but I first had to allow the tears to fall from my face. I first had to let go of the sadness and let go of all the loneliness that hid behind the anger. He instructed me to isolate myself no longer. And then, in a grand slam move, God very clearly and concisely said that it was time to get angry. He assured me in a questioning form through asking the question that I will never forget. The Holy Spirit spoke, "Do not you see that I am the great God of healing? Do not you believe in Me, the Almighty?" So I want to go forth and preach the gospel, *the gospel of purity healing.*

You see, what I went through twenty years ago, society, the world, and even the body of Christ were not ready nor equipped to handle or even begin to talk about in much of any fashion. The issues of sexual molestation were sort of *off-limits* to discuss. Let us take a step back. They were willing to talk about it, but they were not equipped with the *knowledge* or *know-how* in how to untangle the strongholds. I believe that they are better equipped now. I believe that there are certain bodies of Christ whom God has put into place to help such victims of incest. To help guide them in the steps that they need to take to begin their journey to getting whole. I believe God has removed the *stumbling blocks* in a lot of the bodies of Christ and has granted certain *leaders, teachers, and counselors* the wisdom that they need to help victims complete their journey of long-awaited healing.

It has taken a lot of confidence that only God has instilled in me to write this book. For in doing so, I am fully aware that criticism can be thrown out there, appearing as a two-edged sword. But there is only one two-edged sword that I rely on, and that is the Word of God. It is the only true two-edged sword that brings healing. If there are words to describe what it was like to walk through this uncharted territory of repressed memory, then I do not have them. What I do have is peace, love, and joy in the Holy Ghost throughout the journey to completion and wholeness.

Kudos

One thing that I will give to Pedis is that they are good negotiators. They find out what the child's unmet needs are, and they wave it over them like a fan. Whether it's prize money, clothing or desperately needing food and shelter, or even a lack of love in the home, leave it to them to figure it out. In addition, they are con artists. The definition of a con artist is someone who cheats or tricks someone by persuading them to believe something that is not true. Another definition is someone who cheats or tricks someone by gaining their trust and persuading them to believe something that is not true. In my particular case, my Pedi tried to persuade me into believing he loved me and that he would be better off as my dad than my real dad and that I needed to stop putting my energies into loving my real dad and give all of my love to him. Because after all, who clothed you, who fed you and sheltered you? These are the statements he would repeat over and over to me. Love was his commodity, along with a good, healthy paycheck that he used to provide my family with a nice home.

A Pedi looks for the *lack* in a child. Say they are lacking in your basics like clothes or food, they will quickly step in and provide that to them. *To fill in the void of that child's need.*

In my case, these were basic parenting responsibilities that were not being fulfilled by my own mother.

It is alarming if you think about it that a Pedi really should get an award in *stalking* because that is what they do before they approach their victim. It is a deeper-seated illness than even most realize. "Illness" is defined as "an *unhealthy condition of body or mind.*"

The other thing that a Pedi looks for is a sign of previous trauma, either sexual, physical, or mental. It is not always the case, but it makes their part easier because they do not have to break down as many walls because their walls have already been broken down for them through no fault of the child.

In my case, there were numerous traumatic incidents that made me prime prey for a Pedi. The loss of my real father's presence in my life was very painful. I was very sad and solemn. My mother hated my father so bad that this Pedi was able to convince my mom to separate us from the presence and visitation of my dad for two years. Even at the expense of illegally changing our real given last name to the Pedi's last name when enrolling us in school. Charade. Those were the two years that the most damage took place. When the Pedi had more freedom to roam because my real dad was not in close proximity.

The severe burns that I suffered made me feel helpless, hopeless, and fearful at all times. I was an open territory, primed and ready for anyone to take over and love me. I was like a sitting duck, wounded in my brokenness. You can read more in depth about this part of my life in my first book, *Hollow Family Tree*.

Another traumatic incident that happened in my early childhood was that I survived the watching of the crib death of my baby sister. This was especially detrimental to me, as I was the one who heard her cries for help and was unable to get my mom to respond quickly enough to help her. Being the good girl that I was, I knew better than to break the rules and enter her room to help her. I carried the guilt of her death with me for far too many years, and I am sure that it was quite visible in my demeanor when the Pedi was seeking his prey. Yet another *family of origin* breakdown.

You could even call them, in some ways, illusionists. They have a way of *shushing you* and *shutting you up* and making things *appear* differently than they truly are. Or making things *like purity disappear* as mine did. Making you feel like you needed to just withdraw emotionally and not exist unless called upon. They have a way of imparting a depth of fear that is different from what the average child would think of as fear. They emotionally reel you in, and as they are doing it with each crank of the wheel, they con you into believing that you want it too.

The fact that this mind trip is being perpetrated on a child's undeveloped thoughts and emotions is extra traumatic than if done to a mature adult. A child is learning through each circumstance when they are growing. When they have such systematic victimization, their thought process gets warped. There goes that *tainted window* again.

If you think about it, in the spirit realm, the Pedi does not call on the power of God in their life; they call instead on the power of darkness.

So to say that a Pedi is like a magician is not far off from the truth. You see, they magically (a word that I seldom use in my life) convince you that everyone is your *enemy* excluding themselves from the equation. That everyone is against you and they are not on your side but that they, the Pedi alone, are your only true companion. They alone are your confidant. They alone are your fixer and helper. They alone can make everything better. They alone are your only hope, and you need them to feel better. Insanity.

My Pedi used to say, "Come to Daddy. Come sit on Daddy's lap. Daddy will make it all better." And before you know it, you do not trust anybody but that Pedi. Any secrets between the two of you (a.k.a. sexual molestations you would not dare confide in anybody because, after all, they have taught you that others are your enemy) are kept just that...*secret*.

Pedis are good readers of people. It is a form of mind control. I believe that they use the powers of the dark side to develop their abilities to read people. They can tell if you are slipping away emotionally. If they see you taking a step back from trusting them, then they incite fear by way of threatening you. Scaring you. Scaring you with their threats. They threaten you with such scary consequences if you ever tell. They play on your likes and your dislikes.

They pay close attention to what comes out of your mouth about you. They then take your own words, and they play them back at you at your point of weakness or of questioning their actions. This brings on *confusion* in your mind. They use this *confusion as a weapon*. The Pedi needs to gain complete control before they proceed any further with the acts of molestation upon you. They begin to creepily add to just a little bit of what you have said, to change it, just enough to slant it over into their corner of the conversation, inevitably granting them control of what you say.

In my older sister Kathy's particular case, our Pedi was able to convince her to tell my mom that she was *lying* about being molested by him. Therefore, I say that the Pedi uses the powers of darkness to obtain and achieve their goal. It is very similar to brainwashing. Now that is scary.

While it should be our heart that all might be saved, make no mistake, God very clearly speaks that He hates wickedness. The only time He will really do anything for the wicked is when He sees the wicked trying to come against His people, His holy ones. It is then that God will step in and *stop the wicked from harming His chosen*, and even then, He is selective. Something I have never been able to fully understand.

"The Lord trieth the righteous: but the wicked and him that loveth violence his soul hateth" (Psalm 11:5).

The act of sexual abuse is violent. The Pedi tries to act as if what they are doing to you is a good thing. They are so twisted in their mind that they think that you like it. That they are bringing you joy. They are so sickly in need of love and to be loved that one has to say, "What happened to that person in their childhood to make them act like that?" It is horrific.

The Lord began to show me that *I have a voice*. A voice that comes from this *experience* and that I am to *speak my truth* and that nobody can take that away from me through their theology or their explanations of what I firsthand experienced! It is in *speaking out in truth* against the Pedi's behavior that I would begin to understand first handily for myself how much emotional pain he had inflicted upon me. It is when we stay *closed in the closets of our mind* that the strongholds gain power. In the speaking out, the darkness must flee in Jesus' name.

"They shall go with their flocks and with their herds to seek the Lord; but they shall not find him; he hath withdrawn himself from them" (Hosea 5:6).

You cannot hurt God's children and think that you can just simply repent, and all is well in the house of the Lord. I have heard the term from many people—preachers included—that has always disagreed with my spirit that sin is sin. There is a difference in molesting a child and stealing a candy bar from a store. Both are sins, but both are dealt with on different heavenly levels of punishment.

The Lord knows the way of the righteous, and He also knows the way of the ungodly and the wicked. Psalm 1:6 says that the ways of the ungodly shall perish. Stand up for righteousness at all costs, for God is able.

I have tried to write this book with as much dignity as possible, knowing that it would affect different people in different ways, but also knowing that the truth needed to be exposed. The way of the righteous shall prosper and increase. At times I did not think so. I knew that God was leading me to tell my story, and He kept encouraging me to stand up for righteousness at all costs. He would speak to me that He was not a man that He should lie. And He promised me that in the end, I would prosper. I see now that what He meant was emotionally prosper. That I would find emotional, solid ground. Solitude.

Finding my emotional voice would take time. What the Pedi does is that he strikes when you are least prepared. They have everything all arranged and organized and manipulated, but you are just a child. You do not think in that capacity of manipulating and coning. You are just existing, trying to live day by day in some sort of joy.

You know the first three fruits of the spirit are love, joy, and peace. Those are the three things that the Pedi tries to rob from you. They try to replace the God in your life and become the source of your love, joy, and peace, all because they are lacking in these three areas themselves.

Instead of going to God to obtain these things, they try instead to steal them from a child. They try and extract them. Even as a child, I would pray to no other. I would talk to no other. Nor sing to no other except Jesus. They try and get you in the place of a subservient. I refused. Even at a young age, I would tell myself how sick he was. I convinced myself that if he were not sick, then he would not be doing this to me. I knew enough on the inside that he was emotionally ill. I had received love from my dad. He was a cool dad. I had that to compare it to, and he just did not compare to anything that a dad should be. This is when I first started calling him *weirdo*.

Being molested, especially when it is being done over and over again, robs the child of loving honestly. It is interesting to me that one of the highest callings in life is to walk in love. The very thing that a Pedi tries to rob from you. Loving others has truly been a rugged journey for me. For in loving, I have had to obey God. I thought that obeying God would always be first and foremost on my heart; however, when God commands me to love someone who I don't even like or can't even stand to be around, it is hard for me to obey Him. It is usually through many sleepless nights that I yield and admit my wrong thinking and then finally submit. I had a deep wound or ditch in my soul that was filled with hate and distaste for this man. God still called me to submit myself, my soul, my ways, and my will and that in doing so, the devil would flee from me. After all, was not the ultimate goal to be free from the devil's grip so that I *could* freely love others?

In the process of filing a civil suit against my Pedi, in a very peculiar way, whispers from the Lord kept coming loud and clear into my ears, convincing me *not to hate* any longer. It was the most extraordinary event. Here I was trying to understand the sickness of a Pedi, and God was more concerned about my heart getting even harder toward the male species. On the other hand, God was assuring me that *no evil deed goes unpunished*. He explained to me that He was the punisher and I was not. Try swallowing that during what I was experiencing!

I wanted him to go to jail. I think that is where he belongs. I think that they need to make a certain prison where just sexual predators and Pedis go. If they want to hurt anyone, they can hurt themselves, but they will no longer hurt children.

I kept clinging to this most awesome scripture:

"But the natural man receiveth not the things of the Spirit of God: for they are foolishness unto him: neither can he know them, because they are spiritually discerned" (1 Corinthians 2:14).

While I knew that God was all goodness, all kindness, all tenderness, and all love, I often questioned His wisdom. I do not think that it is healthy to question the wisdom of God, but it is the place that I was at. In looking back, I now understand how God was doing things. He wanted me to be *set free*, and in doing so, He wanted me to *set free* my Pedi and hand him over to the throne of God. Release.

"But he that doeth wrong shall receive for the wrong which he hath done: And there is no respect of person" (Colossians 3:25).

God Hates Strong Drinks

In the gathering of all my information about Pedis, in what I thought was useful info, it is most prevalent that most all of them use some sort of mind-altering substance. To this day, I have a strong distaste in my mouth for alcohol. It is as if they try and put a backup plan in motion should they ever get caught. They blame the substance, alcohol or drugs; it made them do it. I have known a lot of people through the years who were substance abusers who were not Pedis, so that is a crock.

The Bible refers to strong drinks in the same context as spirits, etc. I can see repeatedly when reading through the Word how alcohol caused people of the Bible to make bad choices and wrong decisions. Even to the extent to where they sold their own children into prostitution (Joel 3:3). I thank God that in all this that has happened, He kept me from the disease and use of alcohol even to the extent of me despising it.

In Jeremiah 33:3, it says to call out unto the Lord, that He will answer thee. He will show you great and mighty things that we know not. While what this Pedi did to me was certainly not great or mighty, the voice that I now stand on at sixty years old is great and mighty. While going through the trauma of remembering these repressed memories, I did not feel so great and mighty, but God knew all these years later that speaking out would make me strong. Would make me the *watchman* that He had called me to be.

Over and over again, with regards to my family of origin, I have been called to stand up for righteousness and have done right standing things to and for my family. Through all of this, they have falsely accused me of much. They mocked me. Satan laid siege to have my soul, but God's *outpouring love won instead.* I have nothing but adoration and a yearning to understand the heart of God. If He was telling me to forgive and to love, then I was to obey and to listen intently with detail so that when this was over, I could walk in health, wholeness, and ultimate healing. In 3 John 1:11, the Bible teaches us:

"Beloved, follow not that which is evil, but that which is good. He that doeth good is of God but he that doeth evil hath not seen God."

It was not hard to convince myself that God would plead my cause and that He would fight against them that war against me. It is my firm belief that there is no justifiable way that Pedis know Christ, for everything that they stand for is contrary to Christ. Much needed mercy.

Blind Eye No More

Mothers, teach your children well. Teach your children that there are bad people out there. Stranger danger is how we teach it in our house. While we joke around about it in a sarcastic, humorous way, it is serious stuff. Teach your children well. Let them know the warning signs. There is more *that* a child needs to know than just *do not take candy from strangers*. Children need to learn to listen to that inner knower that they are all born with. *If something feels off, then it probably is.* If something feels awkward, step away quickly. While you do not want to teach your child to be neurotic, you also do not want them to be naïve and end up in harm's way.

For me, I kept telling God that something must be done about this. This is so wrong. Children do not deserve to be hurt like this. God would speak back to me as spoken of in Jeremiah 44, that the Pedis *serve gods who they do not even know.*

We as parents need to teach our children about the spiritual aspect to the world we live in. Teach them how to pray and in whose name to pray in, the name of Jesus. We cannot always be there to protect them, but we can teach them how to sense and know in their innermost being when something is just wrong. We can listen to and acknowledge their feelings and intuition. We can teach them about the *gifts of the Spirit* as well as the powers of darkness that try and come against those very gifts so that when a child is approached or surrounded by anything that feels or senses dark, they will know to flee and get help. If we do not arm our children with this knowledge that we have, then we are knowingly sending them out into a war with no weapons. If their defenses are down, then that is when the Pedi strikes. He looks for the broken fences around a child and not a child whose fences are up and whose gate is closed.

Divine Delays

I believe strongly in divine delays and that God ordains everything. When I get stalled or postponed for one reason or another, I have learned to just take a step back or take a different road. *To listen to God's whispers.* I have learned full well that God is protecting me and providing safety for me. *Divine delays are created to keep you from evil and to reset you to walking in God's timing.* They have happened to me so many times that I have lost count at this point in my life. After such occurrences, God has shown me numerous times what He has been delaying me for, the prevention of car accidents, running into just the right person in the store, or even avoiding a particularly evil person. Each time I am filled with gratefulness at what a marvelous God I serve.

We need to become more in tune with the spiritual atmosphere that we are living in and put a stop to ignoring, dismissing, and discounting the knowledge that God gives to us in each specified situation. This knowledge is there to protect us. Stay sober-minded, with a listening ear ever ready to hear from God what it is He wants to speak. Let God be your protector. You can trust Him.

Deceptive Happiness

It was difficult for me once I had walked through the memories to watch the life that I was living imploding and looking over to see my Pedi having a successful career and presumably happy life. He thought that he could just pick up the phone and make a quick apology phone call, putting me back in my little corner, and he could just get away with continuing his destructive path of a life. I struggled to just release him over to the Lord. It was a tug of war like no other. I am a fixer. It is by nature what I do. It is ingrained in me. I like to fix problems and make them right. This Pedi was not my problem any longer, or for that matter, his issues never were my problem. It is his sickness. His illness. His soul tie bound problem.

God assured me that he who has hardened himself against the Lord should not prosper, for hardness against God is not wise. So, while it may have looked like all was fine and well at my Pedi's storefront, I knew that what I was seeing was deeply exaggerated. *That he was an evil servant disguising himself as a lamb with no impurities.* Deception. Get him, God. "I release him to You" is what I said. You can have him. He was never mine to begin with. I did not start this problem, but You alone can finish it.

Walking in the counsel of the ungodly is not where I wanted to be. There are seductive, seducing dark angels who live in and around a Pedi and the Pedi's life. They serenade the Pedi, encouraging him to pursue his prey. Convincing him that he has the right to involve a child in his sexually perverted charades.

Once I began to really understand that in the *speaking out,* God was delivering me from any hold that the marionette puppet string-puller had on me, then I knew that I wanted no part in the counsel of the ungodly. For their ways are not God's ways, nor should mine be ungodly either. Allowing the enemy to draw me in one string tighter at a time was not going to happen any longer. I had to release him over to the *mighty hand of God*, cutting any last strings that might be remaining. For I myself sometimes have lived foolishly and extremely disobedient, deceiving only myself. While I was not a Pedi myself, I certainly was locked into the strongholds of the devil. My only way out from all this emotional pain that being molested had caused me was to let go of the hate and the fear.

The Righteous Will Not Be Forsaken

While I had never tried to commit suicide, subtle thoughts of suicide had crossed my mind more times than I care to admit. Being the strong believer in the Word of God that I was, I was knowledgeable enough to know that those were not my thoughts. They instead were spirits of oppression trying to mimic themselves as if they were my thoughts.

Even as a young girl, each time that he would molest me, when he was done with his violation, I would feel so ugly. In the ugliness, it invited the spirit of suicide enough so that it felt welcome to hang around for a few days. I felt so lonely. I felt so isolated and alone and abandoned. All the things that the Pedi had told me that I was. I would think maybe he was right after all and that nobody would want me. I welcomed death, thinking it could be my friend and I would be relieved from the pain.

In all of this revelation that God was giving to me about what I needed to do about these emotions against the Pedi, the one thing that was forefront on my mind was that when all of this was done and over with, I had a life. A life that I was more than willing to get back to living. I knew that God had taught me in His Word:

> *The steps of a good man are ordered by the Lord: and He delighteth in his way. Though he fall, he shall not be utterly cast down: for the Lord upholdeth him in His hand. I have been young, and now am old; yet have I not seen the righteous forsaken, nor His seed begging for bread.*
>
> Psalm 37:23–25

I knew that for me to hold on to the anger against this very emotionally sick Pedi was only going to bring me even more harm. God was assuring me that in His urging and beckoning for me to come back to reality and live was where I needed to be. There was a part of me, and the Pedi was fully aware of this, that in a way was stranded on an emotional island all to myself. In a way, the Pedi had won. The only way that I could turn that *win into a loss* was to obey God's urging and beckoning to come back where I had left off in my mind and to begin to live again as God had originally intended for me to do before this senseless Pedi ever entered my life.

For heaven's sakes, who in their right mind molests a young girl's body, a body that is scared up with skin grafting's that wrapped around to the backside of her body? One very sick person. Holding out hatred against this person was only damaging me. He was already damaged goods who was in dire need of the grace of God. God began to disconnect me emotionally, one electrical outlet at a time. He assured me it was not my grace that he needed because I am powerless without Christ but that it was God's extended grace that he needed. This was out of my control. Control that was eating me alive. Control that needed to be released.

Satan kept telling me that "Strike three, you are out. You are done. You are doomed." But God gently, through His kindness, turned it around and said, "Yeah, you're done; you're done with holding on to the hatred and the bitterness, and now it is time to release him over and into My hands." Homerun.

Gentle Washing

The gentle washing and renewing of my mind through the Holy Spirit's power is what has changed me into the woman of God that I am today. God's meek movement in my day-to-day life is what has caused me to be meek and gentle to others. In times when I have not been so kind, God was able to change my mind through kindness. His kindness far outweighed my kindness. His kindness is supernatural, and it will always trump my earthly ways. His righteousness far supersedes mine, for I am only righteous to God through the eyes of Jesus. I decided that I would stand for godliness and let go of the hatred and step up upon the rock, allowing my deliverer and Him alone to get justice. I refuse to hold my breath and wait for his apology, the one that will never come from a pure and repentant heart. I, instead, will *go forth* as God has so graciously escorted me into doing.

Shame Bound

Let me be perfectly clear, Pedis are not dumb. They use the part of the brain that the average person would use for good, and they use it for evil gain. It is another form of mind control.

They know enough to find a child that is bound by shame already. Because they themselves are bound by shame, it is very easy for them to bear witness to a shame-based child. They begin to try and create an unhealthy soul tie with that child. It is a satanic power soul tie that quiets a child. That hushes a child and mutes the child. They teach you not to tell, and they educate you as to what the consequences will be if you do tell. I believe, therefore, we do not see more children or even adults come forth and expose their Pedis or sexual offenders. While I don't have facts to back it up, again, I say that I believe that a large percentage of Pedis use a mind-altering substance of some sort because they are so sick that they can't even live with themselves in the way that they are acting and harming others.

Another behavior that Pedis have is that they like repetition. They like to zero in on things being repeated. A little bit compulsive obsessive. In my case, things had to be perfectly aligned before he proceeded forth in molesting me. Very methodical. Like a perfectly planned out play. They would make great playwriters. Down to the time of day. Who is and is not home? They already must have scouted out what the end result is that they desire before the play even begins. A lot of times, I would see the play starting up, and I would quickly find a friend's house that I could spend the night at. Escape.

We lived in two different homes while my mom was married to the Pedi. The first home, within no time, he got approval from the landlord to build a fence that surrounded the entire house, all except the front door. His excuse was that it was a busy street. In actuality, he was setting it up so that when my mother would come home, she had to pull up, put the car into park, get out of the car, open the gate, pull the car into the driveway, and then re-latch the gate closed behind here. *Hello, Mom's home!* He repeated the same scenario at the second house that we moved into. They were both six feet tall wooden fences that you could not see through. That is exactly why these types of people belong in prison. They tell you when to get up, when to eat, etc., which takes away all their control. The Pedi's ultimate goal is to get you so tightly wrapped up into their warped soul ties and sick dysfunction that it makes it difficult for you to tell anyone. As a victim, the thought of telling can bring such an awful fear over the child that you cannot even figure out why you cannot bring yourself to tell. You become *soul tie bound*. The shame compounds. Though this may be a little deep, along with the soul tie and his demons with his escort of fear, the satanic fear begins to put chains around your brain to never tell a soul. Now, if that is not devil worship, then I do not know what is. Emotionally paralyzed.

Another form of binding that child up that the Pedi is all too familiar with is that they bind them with their shame. Shame exposed in a child's eyes leads to total destruction, or at least that is what the Pedi convinces the child of. If I felt unloved before this newfound shame, how was I supposed to be any more lovable with it exposed? In the shame binding, they act as if they are doing you a *favor*, helping you out in your life. All of this is *a lie* that the victim gets sucked into.

While Pedis act like they are in control, it is the one thing that they are in the deficit of. They have no self-will to stop themselves, and that is why I call it an illness. They have no control to suppress the temptation to harm. They are in a deep need of emotional help, and they turn that need onto the child to rescue them emotionally. Heavy burden.

Deliverance from Shame

Guarantee yourself that shame attacks your worth. If you are already feeling worthless, then you automatically go in the *deficit worth file*. I believe shame is behind every suicide in America. They may say it's drug overdose and accidental. I believe each one is accompanied by a dose of shame.

The Pedi does not typically try and molest a child who has confidence and two well-rounded and attentive adult parents. No... Pedis are actually weaklings. They look for the broken or weakened vessels, and sometimes, of no fault of your own, the consequences and conditions that you are found in will cause the Pedi to seek you out. Easy prey.

Shame-based at the core, you try to mull along at life, not really understanding that you can be set free from such a deeply seated imbedded emotion. It is called deliverance, not found to be practiced in most churches, yet it is desperately needed. People come to the knowledge and understanding that they are suffering from shame, and yet they most times do not know what to do with the emotion or how to get rid of it. I have seen strong Christian women fall from grace all because they were never able to overcome shame through prayer and deliverance.

There was a move in the late eighties and early nineties regarding shame. Books were written, and talks were given. You could turn the TV channel, and almost every talk show was addressing it. The problem was that though they talked about it, they never really gave a way to be delivered from this very draining emotion.

Consequently, people go on in life ignoring the very dreadful emotion of shame. The more that you ignore it, the deeper and darker that the shame grows and embeds itself within. I believe that most shame starts from abuse and or neglect as a child. Once you acknowledge that you are shame-based and ignore it, shame, when done with its cycle, will consume you. Like sin, when it is played to its end, it brings death. Unaddressed shame will cause you to *act out* in several ways:

Social phobias. You will begin to hibernate if you can get away with it. I had a husband who made good money, and I could stay home if I needed to. This worked against me.

Insomnia. You begin to worry, and worry dwelled upon turns to sin. Sin leads to insomnia. The devil plays on sin.

Deep imbedded loneliness. You begin pushing people away. Before you know it, you have no friends or family around you because you have isolated yourself from others. Once the devil isolates you, he can play you like a fiddle.

OCD behavior. Because the mind will try anything and everything possible to rid oneself from the gross emotion of shame, you possibly will start trying to organize things. Numbers. You may even begin to try things such as lining up all the dishes in your cupboard or counting things as you go about your daily life. All in order to get some sort of order in your emotions.

Shame entangles you and invites many debilitating enemies. Shame makes you feel very uncomfortable in many given situations. Where a whole, sane person would feel comfortable, a shame-based person just feels dirty. Shame can get so deep down into you and under your skin that you feel like no one can understand you. Dirty and vile.

My best suggestion, and it worked for me, is to repent and ask God for deliverance. Ask God for help, no longer trying to fix it on your own. Jesus speaks in John 15, "That I am the vine, and you are the branches that we are to stay connected to the vine." When shame hits close to home, it can be so painful, and you can feel so unclean that oftentimes we take detours down wrong roads or wrong branches looking for some sort of relief from the pain that the shame has brought you.

In my case, I had done quite well in my profession, and prior to the repressed memories surfacing, I had learned how to shop. Shopping made me feel valuable and accomplished. It made me feel as if I had arrived. It made me feel like all the things that people had told me, that I never would amount to anything, that they were wrong, and I was right. Being right is not all that it is cut out to be. Shopping made me feel in control. It made me feel worthful. It made me feel important. It made me temporarily feel like *I had arrived*. When all the memories surfaced and my career was coming to a screeching halt, I no longer had the money to run out and numb with. Suddenly, I was forced to feel these dirty feelings of shame without the ability to wash them away with a flood of shopping bags.

In a very strange way, we become the prodigal son or daughter, and we have to find our way back to the only true vine and be delivered from the very reason in the first place that caused us to take a detour down the wrong road. These strongholds need severing. Shame held onto causes one to become bitter. I began going to the Word of God and searching out the definition of bitterness. I looked up the scriptures regarding bitterness like...

> *Let all bitterness, and wrath, and anger, and clamor, and evil speaking, be put away from you, with all malice: And be...kind one to another, tenderhearted, forgiving one another, even as God for Christ's sake hath forgiven you.*
>
> Ephesians 4:31–32

Follow peace with all men, and holiness, without which no man
shall see the Lord: Looking diligently lest any man fail of the
grace of God; lest any root of bitterness springing up trouble you,
and there by many be defiled.

Hebrews 12:14–15

You see, earlier, I said to repent. While that may not seem logical, it is the only way *out of your shame*. Acknowledging that you have shame and not addressing it is when it becomes sin. To know to do right and to not do it, according to the scriptures, becomes sin (James 4:17). I did not like this recipe for remedy. At this time in my life, I was still in the blame mode. While the Pedi was to blame for what he had done to me, God kept showing me that I was responsible for getting all these bad emotions of shame under the blood. This took me many years. I truly do not know any quick fixes. I do believe in them, though.

In a paraphrase, say that you have an ex-husband. You know that you hate him, and the hate has grown to deep levels. God shows you that the hating is wrong, but you refuse to quit hating; it is really at that point that it becomes sin. I would pray that God would please set me free from any unclean thing in me, around me, or that could be oppressing me. I would read those scriptures over and over and would ask God to deliver me from any and all emotions of feelings of bitterness that I had in my life. I had to admit my sins to the Father, acknowledge that I was bitter, and come to the full acknowledgment that I was standing in need of prayer. God already knew all of this, but He needed me to come to this knowledge. Repentance was on the forefront of my mind. You see, bitterness takes root when you give audience to hatred and jealousy. The jealousy or covertness of what others have that you do not have physically and emotionally or hatred in your heart that you refuse to give up feeling, which is where the bitterness sets in. As a Christian, I was accountable before the Lord to cleanse myself of any impure thing that had me in bondage. I was responsible for getting it under the *blood of the Lamb*. I had no choice if I wanted to feel whole and actually be healed of the shame.

Shame held onto in the end will destroy you. You must *release* the shame to be free from all the little minor inflictions of the sin that have been committed upon you.

Gained Insight

If you are one of those people in the body of Christ who is still in a broken state, examine your heart and be real with God. He is always real with you. He has already sent His own Son Jesus. Jesus is the overcomer. There is a way for ultimate healing all the way down to the pit of your soul; however, it takes an honesty too few are willing to travel. Ask God to *help* you to become willing. I finally became willing.

God waits upon you. He waits for you to become a hundred percent honest with him. For me, it took a lot of years to be completely transparent with God. Unknowingly, I was figuring out in my head things as I would be in prayer. But God just wanted me to enter into prayer with Him and allow Him to lead and for me to follow. It was a lot of depth at times. More depth than any doctor could help me through or was able or willing to go through. I could not seem to understand why I could not just enter prayer and worship and praise and that that would be that. I was like, *Come on, God, I know that I was molested. Can't You just heal me of it instantly*? But no, God wanted to take me far deeper than I could ever believe or wonder on my own. He had a plan for my life. He wanted me whole. Not partially whole. He was looking for one hundred percent of me. I knew that I was a wounded warrior for Christ. But I figured that it was better to be halfway whole than none at all. God, in His infinite love and concern for me, *wanted all of me*. Even my woundedness.

I was so ashamed of my darkened soul. Weighed down by oppression, sexual abuse, and neglect that I would try and hide a part of me when I would enter prayer. But was I really? God saw through it all. Truly, I figured that I was healed emotionally, as far as I could be, but not with God... He never does anything halfway. Now He may give you a half time, a reprieve, a break if you will, but then when you least expect it, when you are looking in a different direction, He gently ushers you back down the same road and oftentimes the one that you may have just traveled down just a few days or a few years before. He takes you there where you left off in your healing journey. He never leaves you. We instead leave God.

I found that by allowing God to help me to finish out a given situation, a problem, an offense, or an area of mass destruction within my soul, I could finish up in prayer with Him, open up my eyes and go back to life as usual, and the feeling inside of me would be healed. It was amazing. As opposed to standing stubbornly while in prayer with my eyes closed yet unwilling to just relax and allow God's Spirit to guide me down into the shadow of the valley of death and to heal my darkened-gray soul. A soul that was filled with tar and unforgiveness. I did not always understand this concept or movement of the almighty God; I just figured that in my point of prayer, with my eyes closed, it should be all light and fluffy and gleeful. Well, this was not so. Not when I had unresolved hatred, disconnect, and discontent within me. Darkness disconnects you from God. Even darkness perpetrated against you can disconnect you from God's holiness. I thought I had fully surrendered over to God. Much to my *know-it-all personality*, my journey into ultimate healing had only just begun. God was going to have it His way or nothing at all. He has the final say.

You see, the scars from being molested were deeper than I ever even realized. Especially since I had repressed them. They sat idle for all those years. Boy, was I in for a rude awakening. God had spoken many different words to me at many different times in my salvation walk, yet it took me years to realize that most of those words *were for me* and *my own healing*. I journaled, and I wrote for over thirty years. Often, I would go back and reread what I had written, and I could not thank God enough for the revelations as I would read. While I could not a lot of the time find any material out there to help me, God would miraculously create it just for me by my own hand being submitted under the anointing of the Holy Spirit.

I knew that I was intentionally supposed to address certain issues that I had written about. You see, my spirit was born again, and when I would write with my hands, I would surrender it over to the Holy Spirit because I was filled with and baptized in the Holy Spirit, and yes, with the evidence of speaking in tongues. So, as I would write certain, things would come forth through my own hands. Great revelations would surface. I would reread at a later date portions that I had written, and the mind of Christ within me would reveal through my writings areas that I needed to enter into in prayer. I needed to ask God to complete the healing work within me that He had once started. Peculiar yet affective, I know, but does it not say in God's Word, "Ye are a peculiar people of a royal priesthood..."?

> *But ye are a chosen generation, a royal priesthood, a holy nation, a peculiar people; that ye shall shew forth the praises of him who hath called you out of darkness into his marvelous light: Which in time passed were not a people, but are now the people of God: which had not obtained mercy, but now have obtained mercy.*

> 1 Peter 2:9–10

He had brought me out of the darkness of the repressed memory and into the marvelous truth of His light. He began to assure me that everything was going to be all right. Amen, Jesus!

This journey of ultimate healing took on a story in and of itself. Anyone looking on might think that I was a different species. Well, I am. I am truly converted for Christ, one hundred percent, Holy-Spirit-filled, on fire,

NO MORE SKELETON WINTERS

outspoken, a truth carrier, a bluntly mannered woman of God. I deserved ultimate healing all the way down to the very bottom of my soul. God completed the work in me that He had started. God had sustained me.

From the first day of my salvation, God would draw me to His Word. All I owned was an oversized family Bible when I first got saved that came with the big set of encyclopedias that the door-to-door salesman tried to sell to me with a payment plan. God was working ahead of schedule in my life. There is no way I would have bought that Bible being unsaved, but He knew enough to find a way to get it into my house for when I would so desperately need it. Miraculous. You should have just seen me toting that clunker of a Bible around at my first invite to a Bible study. Ha-ha. Within two weeks, the leader of the home Bible study handed me my new, more practical, blue leather-bound Nelson Bible. Cherished.

You see, God knows my heart, and He knows your heart. He knows you inside and out far more than we know ourselves. He knows our hurts and our suffering. I would read the Word faithfully and continually. Anyone looking on would wonder if maybe I was reading the Bible too much, but it was in the reading of *God's Holy Word* that He would draw me into prayer. It was in the continued pattern of obedience that God would take me to those secret places while in prayer. Places that He wanted to heal within me. It just took me a little while to walk through them all.

I believe now, as I have aged, that God had and has a *special anointing* that He has chosen for me to carry. That I am to carry His presence. That I am to bring it forth the message of ultimate healing and divine love to those that have been harmed. I say "who have been harmed" because it includes many offenses. It includes those who are wounded both internally and externally. Those who have lost a breast due to burning on fire and those who have lost a limb in battle for our country. It includes those who have lost their self-esteem due to being raised by a Pedi stepfather or having a real father who was absentee due to divorce. Once you are wounded, you need to be healed. It was going to require crying and tears. Tears that should have been shed many years ago, but unfortunately, in my family line of dysfunction, tears were not acceptable. *Only babies cry.* Now it was my time to be that baby and cry before the Lord. Babies, it is.

> *For as many as are led by the Spirit of God, they are the sons of God. For ye have not received the spirit of bondage again to fear; but ye have received the Spirit of adoption, whereby we cry, Abba, Father.*
>
> Romans 8:14–15

I tried counselors, psychologists, ministers, psychiatry, and self-help groups, all of which added a portion to my healing, but ultimate healing came through much time of being broken before God and trusting that my ultimate needed healing can and will be completed. If you have had many stacked upon offenses occur to you or done to you, then you can be certain that it is going to take a little longer. God has a road to healing for everyone, saved or unsaved. Some roads are shorter and quicker, and that's cool; congratulations; however, if your road appears to be longer, do not allow anyone to tell you any different. But rather listen to the voice of God. Not everyone who says "Lord" shall enter into the kingdom of heaven (Matthew 7:21). In other words, if you have pain still resonating on the inside of you, then you still need to dig deeper. If you are listening to people vs. the Holy Spirit, if you are just sitting in church and listening to the church service rather than taking the sermon and throughout the week living the sermon up with the Holy Word of God, well, then you are possibly listening to the wrong voices. Who are you really listening to?

There is a topic that God began to show me when I was in my thirties. He would say to me, "Premature forgiveness." I sought Him out in prayer regarding these words many times. God began to speak to me through His Word and other biblical teachings that premature forgiveness does no one any justice.

Understanding Premature Forgiveness

This is an area of the Christian lifestyle that I have butted heads with many people. Even rooted Christians many times.

Forgiveness. Wow, it is a difficult thing to walk graciously in. Especially when people have harmed you, despitefully spoken evil against you, and intentionally used you with only evil and darkness as their motive, and after forgiving them, they continue to repeat the same behavior over and over again against you. For me, God was showing me how to avoid the pitfalls of premature forgiveness. You see, if you prematurely say, "I forgive that person for the wrong that they have done to me," before analyzing why it was that they harmed you in the first place, then *it* is actually immaturity on your behalf. I believe the Bible clearly identifies your responsibility as the forgiver. It is your responsibility as a believer in Jesus Christ to hold the offender, the Pedi, to the truth of what it was that they did to offend or hurt you. If a deep, deliberate wound was intentionally created, then it is your duty to protect yourself from allowing this offense to occur against you again if it is within your power to stop it. Otherwise, you hold some accountability for allowing this behavior cycle to continue.

"If it be possible, as much as lieth in you, live peaceably with all men" *(Romans 12:18).*

While you are not God, you are a carrier of God's Holy Spirit and of God's presence. If you allow the offender to continue harming or hurting you and you quickly accept their apology, yet they turn around and cause the offense again, then you are really the one standing in need of prayer because the Word of God says:

"Saying, Touch not mine anointed, and do my prophets no harm" (Psalm 105:15).

So if you forgive prematurely before the offender is made aware of why it is that they continue to harm you, then what are you really achieving? You must ask yourself, in a strange way, are you allowing them to harm you? Codependency at its finest.

Say, for example, you have a friend, one that you know loves God, yet this friend gossips to some of your mutual friends that you both share. You hear of it, and you go to this friend and confront them, and they say that they are sorry. You say, "Oh, I forgive you." In reality, you hold part of the blame in this situation because to truly forgive this friend, as both of you are Christians, you actually need to get to the bottom of the whys that they felt compelled to speak gossipy about you in the first place. What part of the dynamic of this relationship do you have a responsibility for? Covering up unforgiveness never lasts long. If you do not get to the heart of the issue, then chances are that that friend will just repeat the same cycle. This inner mingles with the cycle of addiction. As well as inner links with premature forgiveness.

Interlinkings

Okay, let us take it deeper. Say you have a husband who hides his sinful actions behind your back. Perhaps he has a gambling addiction. Maybe God has helped him with this addiction in the past, and you catch him using the internet to place a bet. You confront him about it, and he admits to having been gambling for months. Now that he is confronted, he promises to stop again.

As a wife, what are you offended by? That he lied to you? That he stole money and hid money that was jointly yours? That he compromised his integrity again? It could be several reasons that you are feeling betrayed or manipulated. For you to say "I forgive you..." prematurely, you are enabling him to repeat the old behavior. As a wife, mate, and friend, you have an integrity issue, first and foremost, that you ethically should not brush under the rug. If it is the umpteenth time that you have caught him in a predicament of compromised integrity, then if you just jump in with both feet with forgiveness, you are part of the problem.

Idle Tongue

Say you have a mother who speaks behind your back to your siblings or a father, either way, and you know that they are continuing to gossip and even make up things about you just to spread more lies to your siblings, almost as if they enjoy running you into the ground. You finally muster up enough courage to try and forgive them. Here is the problem, how can you sincerely forgive when you know the pain within you is much deeper than an "I forgive you"? This is what I am talking about regarding premature forgiveness. I have done it way too many times. Repeatedly. What God was showing me was that in many different situations of my life where there has been emotional abuse and where victims have been raised in this abuse, when the victim comes to Jesus and the abuser remains out in the world unsaved, it is few and far between that the one abused can say that "I forgive you."

Rather, *it is a process*. It is not something to take lightly either. It is also something that you *cannot* honestly say one time, "I forgive you too." The layers and layers of lies, hurt, and real pain that need to be picked through can take years. It is a healing process, and yes, while forgiveness is the remedy, it is not the cure. *Love is the cure.* Love obviously does not flow freely from mother to child in the above example. So God must step in and love on the child, the victim. Even when God loves that child, person, or victim, it is only when they *receive* God's love that they become a victor. This can take years for God to soften and massage a heart of stone. Though the victim has been converted for Christ and to Christ, because of their abusive past, it can take a long time for the victim to even know that God is loving on them. Sad...huh? A parent's love is essential for a child to develop normally. Without the love of a mother, people can become many different sad, lonely, and self-destructive things. The love of a mother is something that gets imparted into a child.

Without love, the child suffers a deep-seated loneliness. I believe that this is one of the number one links to suicide in unloved people. Feeling unloved and unwanted and in the way, a burden and a problem, or just another mouth to feed as a child can send that child into forming very self-destructive thoughts and behaviors. This is the reason that when they become adults, even if they are loved, they cannot *feel love*.

When a victim of abuse begins a relationship with God that in and of itself is miraculous, let us give God credit where credit is due. What a miracle that that broken person is not so consumed with anger with God that they do not even want anything to do with Him and what He has to offer, eternal life. When that victim does finally turn to Christ, they really do not understand the love of God. It is just a concept to the victim that mimics a fairy tale that they are reading about in the Bible. One that they certainly do not apply to themselves. When God starts pouring out His love, His blessings, His miracles, His ways on the victim, they cannot for the life of themselves understand why. As a victim, you are thinking, *What is this going to cost me?* So for that victim of emotional or sexual abuse, it takes time. Time for them to get to know God. A God that is so contrary to anything they have experienced. Time to learn how to soak in God's presence.

Learning to be vulnerable is a task. Time to learn how to meditate in His Word, which requires faith, which must be built in trust. Time to wrap their head around the fact that God sent His Son Jesus, who died and rose again so that we might live.

A victim feels guilt once they come to Christ that they get to live. If that victim is blessed enough to eventually come to a place of finally getting to acknowledge who God is, it is then that they might be at the beginning stages of forgiveness.

I think that a large percentage of the body of Christ is uneducated regarding real child abuse, child neglect, stroke deprivation, and child endangerment. I think that it is high time that the true born-again Christians step up to the plate and *go to battle in prayer* for the wounded trapped in childhood abuse so that they can be delivered from their past and join in on *the battlefield for Christ.* Fully equipped to wage spiritual warfare against the devil and all his craft manipulative dark angels.

I personally was one of those children who suffered at the hands of very young, inexperienced, worldly, and rebellious parents. I suffered at their expense. I lacked being loved because I had parents who were not shown love themselves. For them to love meant that they had to give away what they did not have to give, and that would take faith that they did not have, for they were living in the world. Most people who live in the world operate out of fear and not faith. Fear breeds pain. Pain multiplies and turns to despair. Only God, in His *infinite power,* can break through all that darkness. I am writing all of this to say: Let us give these children of abuse a little room and a little time to forgive. Honest forgiveness. Let us not judge them because they need to walk through all the vomit that has happened to them or been placed upon them. Let us allow them the steps that they need to take before they can come to a full honest forgiveness from the depths of their soul.

Sometimes in the Christian realm, church, we are uncomfortable even beginning a thought of what a victim has gone through. We most often want to give them a quick fix answer. A scripture. A cure. A spiritual Band-Aid. When it is rather *patient love* that is the cure. It is time that they need to heal and restart. Time is a cure in and of itself. Let us have some compassion on the bruised and the wounded. Therefore, they do not come to church. They get judged by the body. Very little compassion is to be found. I happened to be able to play the part to fit in on the outside, wear the right clothes, being raised with manners to learn how to mimic different scenarios in life. It was one big bad cover-up. It did not work. I would still leave feeling deeply wounded. Trapped in a ball of confusion.

Let us not try and put a skin graft over a deeply imbedded wound. You will end up trapping the wound and giving it no place to breathe, which can cause the wound to get infected and be unable to heal. Let us give these victims a way that they can feel safe to speak out and tell their story so that they can get it *out* of them. So that they can be healed of painful, destructive memories. Unless we allow God to go all the way down to the bottom of the soul and heal their land, heal their life, their soul will become dark and remain full of unbelief that God does love them and that God does know them.

God knows that you have an unrepented, unresolved hatred and unforgiveness down in the depths of your soul; however, God is willing if you are willing to walk through the valley of death. He will walk with you so that you will fear no evil thing. Behind all unforgiveness is fear. Sometimes the healthy Christian is just that very person that God needs to step up to the plate, to be used of Him to assist in the victim's life, so that they may become a victor in Christ. You may need to be *love in the flesh* to that person until they can accept the true fact that God loves them. This, for me, was a much longer process than I would have wanted it to be. Time and time again, I would be in conversation with a person, and I would try to express what I was feeling or walking through with very little understanding coming back at me. There was compassion at times but minimal understanding of child abuse. What a toll it takes on a person's mind. The devil plays on that person's mind and heart due to lack of Bible knowledge. Let us try and be a little bit more compassionate for the newly found Christian in our churches.

Where Is the Point of Deliverance?

Who is going to speak out to and for these broken people so that they may receive deliverance? Who is going to take the time to explain to them that deliverance must take place for them to be free?

I am a blessed survivor. God very graciously and carefully walked me step by step through several deliverances over the period of thirty-five years. None were too pretty. All were accompanied with tears, sweats, and shakes. All were done for the edification of my soul and performed by the Lord.

I happen to be a very strong personality type. A persistent God-fearing person. So what about that more complacent person? Or, God forbid, a person who has suffered far worse than I did. In the Word, it says that:

> *If my people, which are called by my name, shall humble themselves, and pray, and seek my face, and turn from their wicked ways; then will I hear from heaven, and will forgive their sin, and will heal their land.*

2 Chronicles 7:14

In this scripture, I believe that the reference to the word "land" is talking about the individual and their innermost being. You can't go back and change it, your past that is, but you can learn how to enter into prayer on a fast, covered by the blood of the Lamb, and walk back through the pain, receiving healing. When you do it with God holding your hand as He walks through it with you, then your spiritual eyes will be opened, and strength will arise. God can and will show you that He was with you all the time. You just could not see Him or feel Him in your situation because, at the time, you had a heart of stone that was helping you survive. But now, you have a heart of flesh, which allows you to see through the situation spiritually for the first time in your life. God's love never fails, and nothing can separate you from the love of God.

> *For I am persuaded, that neither death, nor life, nor angels, nor principalities, nor powers, nor things present, nor things to come, nor height, nor depth, nor any other creature, shall be able to separate us from the love of God, which is in Christ Jesus our Lord.*

Romans 8:38–39

Once you know God's love, you can pass it forward. As you give it away, He will replenish you with even more. If you notice in the scripture above, it talks about principalities and powers. The very forces that were used to harm you want to continue to keep you in bondage to your past. When I say, "Where is the point of deliverance?" I am saying that there must be a turning point in one's life where you walk away from the pain, leaving it at the altar, surrendering the pain over to God because you cannot carry it. You have tried to carry it, and where has that gotten you? Has it caused you to remain in darkness in certain areas of your life? There comes a time in each victim's life that deliverance is mandatory. Just ask David of the Bible. He was constantly going to the altar and asking God for deliverance.

Rise Above the Darkness

For several years now, the Lord has spoken this word to me, "*My people perish for lack of knowledge*" (Hosea 4:6). It saddens me that the large portion of the body of Christ and the church does not teach how to get untangled from the powers and principalities of darkness that have victims so tightly bound. There are a few churches in our country that have stepped up to the plate to carry the mantel with regards to deliverance and teaching and empowering the sheep of God in how to walk untangled no longer. I think that we gloss over the true biblical fact that there is *a devil seeking whom he may devour*. It is imperative for the victim of incest or molestation that they find their point of deliverance. Everyone's point of deliverance is different. God appoints the times and the seasons. But make no mistake, we all have one. It is whether we elect to submit to the time and place that is chosen for us.

When the hand of deliverance is placed upon your life, a *wellspring of joy, peace*, and eventually learning to love others comes out of you. Now the trusting part, you know the part where you learn to trust others, for me took a little bit longer, and I am still working on it. I encourage you while you are reading this book that you pose the question to God, "Where is my point of deliverance?"

My next step was forgiving. I could not forgive. I had tried to forgive. So I began asking God *why, why I could not forgive people, situations, and issues.* He showed me that I could not forgive because I needed to get to the core issue, which was anger. I had to take each situation, each circumstance, and dissect each offense or offended person that I hated or was angry at or jealous or bitter toward and get it figured out. This included the Pedi. None of it really made sense until it did. It was definitely a long process. I had a lot of ungodly, sinful feelings toward a lot of people. Once God brought it all to light that I was dealing with powers and principalities and high places, as it says in Ephesians 6:12, I was able to enter into prayer with the power of the Holy Spirit, and I allowed Him to intercede for me as I submitted my request before the Lord. Often, I would be on a fast. This I have found to help. With prayer times as long as six and seven hours in between answering the door, as my grandchildren would come to visit. Life. But I was persistent and continued tarrying in prayer, sometimes day-in and day-out, until this dark satanic force began loosening its grip. Oh...the power of the wonderful name of Jesus. Shame no more.

Now, if anger, jealousy, envy, strife, and contention try and make their way into my life, I try my ultimate best to allow the Holy Spirit to fight for me, and I rebuke these attacks in the name of Jesus. I ask God to supernaturally remove it and to give me peace in place of unrest. I strive daily to put on the *whole armor of God* before I get a sip of my hot coffee, as it speaks of in Ephesians 6:11 so that we may be able to stand against the wiles of the devil.

While I understand victims of incest and pedophilia have already gone through a long and dark road of despair, I still want to encourage you not to shy away from dealing with this issue. But to instead acknowledge *its powers of darkness* that you are coming against and see the full light. Put on your armor and fight for yourself. Find a person that you can confide in that can help you to get through these grueling emotions and put them under the blood once and for all. You can do it.

Everything Comes to a Head

While I was biding my time waiting for my court date to come, which was about six months away, there were many other areas that were also coming to a head. The possibilities of moving were becoming real. I knew that I could not move until my court case was finalized because I did not want to take this trash can of a past along with me on my new beginning. I needed closure.

In conversations with my attorneys, they had already proposed a financial settlement with the defendant's attorney. None of which were acceptable. So I stood my ground and was bound and determined to go forth in a trial and postpone our move. It was not about money anyways; it was about principle: do not touch little children sexually!

The defendant, as of yet, had avoided taking his deposition. He had rescheduled with a mundane excuse for yet another several months. You see, he was banking on the fact that I *mentally* could not handle it; information that was being leaked to him. For him, it was one big extension of the *manipulation and thrill* he received from trying to manipulate me all these years later and still be in control. Just like how he did not show up to my deposition, and I was never told that he would not be there. He *got off* on trying to frighten me; it is what Pedis do.

What I now know, many years later, is that it was my own sister, the Pedi's daughter, that was leaking info to him about what was going on in my life. Sad. There is no other way, no other connections, and no other common link about what was going on with *my life* but through the half-sister. My husband was the one that called this to my attention. This was not an easy fact to accept or to swallow, given how she was the cherished baby that everyone tried desperately to protect. It seemed as if the Pedi and his attorney were always two steps ahead of us. I now know why. Painful but just another example of how he could manipulate and make people believe a lie. It is very sad how in such sick dysfunction, a child will protect the parent even at the expense of losing peace within their own soul. That is codependency at its depth.

Bluegrass Blades

Not much to my surprise, my husband called from work one day, as he had done several times before with different job opportunities. This time, as the words came out of his mouth, it seemed like the right fit.

"Kentucky," he said. "How would you feel about living in Kentucky?"

I replied, "I will let you know in the next twenty-four hours."

The following morning my daughter and I trotted on down to the public library. On our drive, we got a little confused, and we thought he had said Kansas. I remembered the day before when he had said Kentucky that I had connected bluegrass and horses. We realized that we had gotten the state wrong in our mind.

We entered that library with enthusiasm and one goal in mind. To find a handful of books about Kentucky and read up. We each grabbed a few and began whispering back and forth over the table with excitement with each new fact that we discovered.

There was one big catch, which was that I had to get through this court case. I was weighing all my options: the strength of my marriage, the strength of my emotions, how much more I thought that I could deal with, and *would my boys follow and come along?* Not to mention my husband and what he wanted for his own life and career. He really wanted this trial and court case to be *said and done with.* When the attorneys would recommend settling out of court and not dragging my family through the mud with a trial, it seemed to appeal to my husband. All on board. Here we go again with saving the whole world and losing one's soul. I could feel the strength of my marriage weakening; to lose my marriage would be like losing my own soul. I was in love with my husband. I wanted the best for everyone involved, excluding my Pedi, without compromising truth, the truth of what had happened to me. I had to look at every side of the situation.

My daughter and I returned home from the library with a childlike giddiness awaiting my husband's arrival home from work. This newfound possibility of a job in Kentucky was a day position. A day trader opening. My husband had long been a shift worker. That night my daughter, my husband, and I sat around and discussed all the pros and cons. How long would this job offer be open? Should I agree to take a settlement and just let the Pedi off the hook?

How quickly could I sell my house? Was my daughter willing to move to a new high school in a new state her senior year? Was I finally willing to put the past in the past? Would the Pedi be exposed enough to prevent him from harming again? So many questions, but the only one that really mattered was: What did God want? What was His will for our life? Had I done enough damage to turn an eye toward or open an ear for the district attorneys' ear to be open? Did this whole situation shock him enough with the original threat of imprisonment to finally stop him from harming children? Did it shock him enough to realize that he had better quit touching? That was something that I had to ultimately leave up to the Lord.

We decided that night that my husband would interview with this company and get a feel for the position. Excitement in the air once again. They flew my husband out within five days to be interviewed. It was a quick turnaround. He flew out in the morning and came back late that night.

As my daughter and I picked him up from the airport, he expressed his excitement to make a move in his career. He was excited for what seemed to be an unreal job opportunity. They had offered him a position upon interviewing him, making close to twice as much income as his current salary. That seemed right up our alley, as we were hurting financially.

There was one catch. It meant that I would have to relent and settle out of court or quite possibly drop the entire case altogether.

I contacted my attorneys the following day and told them that I wanted to meet with them. My main objective in this whole case was that the Pedi be revealed for who he really was. My second main objective was for my baby sister to come out of denial about who her father was because she was the one who actively still had contact with him. If she were to have children in the future, then at least her eyes were opened, and it would be her decision if she were to bring her children around him.

Reality hit me again through my husband saying that "You are not the Pedi police. Let it go. You have done enough. It is time for us to look out for our family. Let us put our pieces back together. Let us put Humpty Dumpty back together."

I went into my attorney's office, accompanied by my husband. When we entered the office, both attorneys were sitting there. The atmosphere was full of a lot of excitement on their part. They had just gotten off the phone with the defendant's attorney. He had agreed to settle for an amount that they thought was going to work for all parties. I guess the deposition woke up that defense attorney was what we all surmised. I believe that he realized that this girl was not going away any time soon and that I was telling the truth of what had happened to me.

There was one thing missing. I wanted an admission of guilt in writing. In their dilemma, they picked up the phone right there as we were sitting in their office and called the defense attorney back. While they did not put him on speakerphone, I could still hear the conversation and negotiations going on. As sick as this seems, throughout all the negotiations, which disgusted me by the way, both attorneys right there over the phone were negotiating and discussing what percentage of the dollar amount they would receive as payment with one another. The defense attorney clearly stated that his client would verbally admit to guilt but refused to put *it in writing,* as he feared criminal prosecution. I had to weigh all the odds quickly, as we did not want to wait too long because we did not want my *husband's job offer* to expire and be taken off the table.

I made the uneasy decision that day to take the settlement. I could handle the lack of a written confession. My family and I had already received the lovely verbal confession via the phone recorder many months earlier. The one stipulation that I did stand adamant on was that I refused to sign anything about not speaking up in the future about being molested by him. This was a deal-breaker for me. I knew enough in my knower that one day, not knowing it would take twenty-five-plus years later, I could be strong enough to write a book and tell my side of the story. I also knew that in Galatians 6:7, it says, *"Be not deceived; God is not mocked: for whatsoever a man soweth, that shall he also reap."*

I knew that there was a price that the Pedi would eventually have to pay. I kept this in the back of my head as I continued the journaling of my journey. Literally, within minutes of this agreement, the settlement came across the fax. The secretary unrolled the paper and made a copy on the copier quickly. Rapid, swift, express 101. They needed my signature before I changed my mind. Immediately, they sent it back through the fax to the defendant's attorney's office. Wow. This is what it all amounted to. It felt similar to what mafia money might feel like.

I left the whirlwind of the office that day with my husband hand in hand. We both felt like we had achieved close to our goal. This would have to be enough to satisfy us. Chapter slammed closed, well, sort of.

Final Follow Up

I had gained respect for my doctor. In what would be my last appointment, my doctor encouraged me to continue picking up the pieces of my life, but that this time I was to put them back into their *rightful places*. He had already heard from my attorneys by the time I got to this appointment that we had settled out of court. He appeared glad that this part of my life story had concluded. I had grown to where I really trusted this doctor. After all...he had helped me to such a depth than any other doctor would even have dared to wander with me. They would never dare to even venture out and attempt to deal with this deep-seated dark pain. It always impressed me first of all that it was a *man* that I began to trust, but secondly, how he graciously was able to grab ahold of my emotional hand and lead me back to some sort of wholeness and sanity. Back to reality.

My doctor expressed to me that he wanted me to know how, through the counseling of me, his own faith in God had returned. He had started reading his Bible after many years of it collecting dust on the shelf. He voiced to me that my faith in God was "so strong" and "so real" and "so tangible" that it had penetrated through and affected him and convicted him. That he had a desire to start reading it again.

I sat there dumbfounded and thought to myself, *Was all of this for this one soul to reconnect with You, Lord?* All throughout my many months of counseling, he was the listener, the guider, and the educator. He would explain to me a lot of what my dreams meant in the psychiatric world, and I would come back with what I believed to be my godly interpretation. He would always just look at me, swooping that Beatle bang out of his eye and say, "I never thought of it that way, hmmm, interesting." He would say, "Let me look into that, and I will get back to you."

In one dream that I had shared, I was walking through green pastures. Soaring green pastures of blades of grass being moved by the wind. I explained to him that I had begun studying Psalm 23 and that I felt that there was a *move* in my near future. This day he referred to that dream. "Wow. You really are *moving*, and you are *moving* to Kentucky. You know that that is the bluegrass state, right?" he said. It is so cool to me how God works. He works in mysterious ways; my dad used to say this term like is found in Isaiah.

> *For my thoughts are not your thoughts, neither are your ways my ways, saith the Lord. For as the heavens are higher than the earth, so are my ways higher than your ways, and my thoughts than your thoughts.*

Isaiah 55:8–9

I could see that day that my time here with this doctor was done. God was completing many chapters. I thought to myself that if He could cause this well-renowned psychiatrist to think of Him *again*, to *ignite* his long quenched fire, then quite possibly, I had completed the work that God had called me to do, just not in the way that I thought that it would happen. Funny how life works. It was not as if my doctor was telling me that I had to stop seeing him. He did not quit being my doctor like others had. He did, however, encourage me to put one foot in front of another and take a new chance on happiness again.

He told me to keep using the antidepressant and that I quite possibly would have to use them for the rest of my life because of the extent of trauma that I had suffered. He did feel confident that I would be able to get rid of that little white pill soon.

I thanked him for having an ear to hear. I encouraged him on his journey to seek out the Lord. I assured him that every one of the thirty-dollar copays that he never collected from me would be satisfied upon collection of my settlement monies.

Shock and Awe

There was one door still opened in my mind that needed closure, that sign that I had asked God for. You know, the bonus? Just shortly after my husband's return from the initial job interview in Kentucky, he was called into the office at his work. He was very nervous, as he had just gone on the out-of-state interview and thought that quite possibly somehow his boss had found out. He had seen other people get fired and get escorted out of the building for this same infraction. My husband nervously sat across the desk on high alert. His boss handed an envelope to him across the desk. He had just finished up a three-year traveling project; remember all my lonely nights while he was in Florida? This envelope held an unexpected bonus check. Remember the bonuses that this company does not give? Thank You, God. He never lies. He always comes through. He always does what He says He is going to do. My husband sat in stunned awe as he realized what was happening. Answered prayer. Sign confirmed. Moving.

Conditional Acceptance

Days later, with things headed quickly in the right direction, I knew that we needed to let our boys know that number one, we had settled out of court, and number two, that we had partially accepted a job opportunity in the bluegrass state of Kentucky. The one condition that was on the table was that my husband had agreed, provided his wife and oldest son and daughter could be flown out and given the opportunity to see for themselves firsthand what Kentucky was like.

During his trip to Kentucky for the original interview, my husband had brought a local newspaper home with him. In that newspaper, there was a small few line ad tucked into the real estate section for a home on ten acres that was for sale. I found this ad intriguing, and I was curious to take a look at it. I kept picking the ad back up and reading it. The home was a newly built three-bedroom, two-and-a-half-bath with a huge bonus room over the garage. Something that I was sure we could live with.

Everything came together, and I flew out to Kentucky with my oldest son and daughter to get a feel of the area. Whirlwind. Such a night and day from the fast-paced life I had known in California. My kids and I relished in the differences with every turn of our heads. Prior to the trip, my husband had granted me a power of attorney so that if I felt led, I could put an offer on the intriguing home from the newspaper ad. So I called the banker and asked to see the property.

The banker's assistant whipped us around those old country roads in one swooping turn after another, sending us not so gently tugging against our seat belts, until we wound down the newly graveled road to make the last turn exposing the open fields of green grass surrounding a beautiful white home on the hill. Majestic is what I thought. God really cared for me, and I could see His splendor as I surveyed the land that He was handing me on a platter. My refuge.

We signed a contract with zero good faith deposit on our new home, conditioned upon selling our house in California, of course. We swiftly flew back to California with excitement in the air and adrenaline pumping.

One thing that I know for sure is that God will not give you more than you can handle. I was under immense pressure emotionally. Now that I had signed the settlement paperwork, along with it came an unexplainable release of pressure. It looked like I was going to get to make a move out of the city.

Immediately upon returning home, I mentioned to my neighbor what had transpired. She had always really loved our home and the way that we had dolled it up. If we had a yard sale or redecorated for any reason, she was always quick to claim anything we were getting rid of.

I mentioned to her that I was going to put my house on the market for sale, and right away, she said that she was certain that one of her daughters would want to buy it. Within hours a contract was being drawn up, and the house went into escrow the following day.

From the time that we returned from Kentucky, within three weeks, my family were Kentucky residents in our newly purchased, newspaper-ad home. Whirlwind. Ten acres more land than I had ever seen on any residential property that I had sold in California. In Cali, if you have a third of an acre, you are rolling. There was no time for us to look back or question because God wanted our eyes focused forward. *God is a God of timing.*

Immediately upon landing in our new state of Kentucky, we were given the keys to our new home. Unbeknownst to us, we had purchased it directly from the banker who owned it. He was the loan; he was the bank, so it did not take any time other than a few days of processing a few simple pieces of paper, and we were handed the keys. God can and will move mountains.

I believe that a lot of the reason that things fell into place with the move to Kentucky has, *yes,* to do with God's precise timing, but it also has to do with forgiveness and having your sins under the blood of the Lamb. While I had settled out of court, I had yet to receive any money. The receiving of money had nothing to do with the standard that God wanted to hold me to and the obligation that I had to forgive. Somehow, I connected the two. That God knew my heart, and He also knew my needs. I needed privacy from the public arena, time to heal, and a few seasons to repair my wounded soul. Along with it came a beautiful home and ten acres. I told God, "Thank You very much. I will take it."

I learned quickly why they call it the Bluegrass State. It rains a lot! The raindrops are the size of half-dollar coins a lot of times. When they drop, you feel them hitting your skin, and you must pull your car over on the side of the road when they appear out of nowhere while driving...even when on a freeway.

I learned quickly what a cistern was. I had signed the papers, and there was not a whole lot of time for questions. I knew that God was giving me this property. I figured any dilemmas that came my way I would just deal with them. No more running our water while we were brushing our teeth, ha-ha. Funny how things get ingrained into you. To this day, I do not run water while I am brushing my teeth.

We did not even know where we were, but we knew that God had planted us there. New beginnings always seem to give me a thrill. The thrill was on. Could anyone please point out where the grocery store was in town? I could not seem to find a Ralphs' sign anywhere.

After all the trauma I had gone through in the last two years with this stinkin' court case and all the emotions, fresh air seemed so amazing.

In California living, it seemed like I could not take a deep solid breath of fresh air. Just to walk out on my newly built deck and look at the huge bails of round hay that had been plowed on the backside of my property was just astounding. The cool part was that my children, my daughter, and my oldest son seemed just as filled with wonder at the new adventure. My husband's last day of work at the power company was on a Friday, and he literally started his new job at the new company the following Monday morning. He seemed to really enjoy the change in pace, the beautiful rolling green fields. We all enjoyed how people would wave at you and talk to you. We would giggle at these strangers and count how many waved at us.

On the first big trip to the grocery store that my daughter and I took to stock up, we had to use two carts for all the necessities that we had to get rid of in the move. This was *not* a common occurrence in the small town that we lived in. We were definitely drawing attention with our California ways. It was such a small town that people even said, "Oh, you must be the people who bought the big white house up on the hill," on more than one occasion. Bizarre. We quickly learned as we stood there this first trip that we needed to bag our own groceries in this small town. My daughter always thought she would like to work as a bagger, so she finally got her opportunity, just not with pay.

I had made a covenant between the Lord and me that if there was pain that He needed me to continue walking through, then I would, but I was going to minimize the time that I spent thinking about the civil case that I had just settled out of court with. It was not something that I was ashamed of, but it was not something that I was going to tell people about either. I was becoming a new creature in Christ. I was beginning to feel joy that I had never experienced in my entire life. The antidepressants seemed to be doing their job. I was determined to just plow forward and do my best to not look back.

Compounded Interest

There was very little conversation between my old attorneys and me. They would periodically contact me, usually about once a month, and explain to me how they were unable to get the defendant to pay me the settlement amount that he had agreed upon and explain how our case seemed to be stagnant.

Along about the eighth month after settling, I received a phone call from my attorney. He explained to me that they were going to file the proper paperwork with the courts asking for the highest allowable interest rate to be tacked onto the already agreed upon civil settlement. Interest that would compound itself by the day. For each day that he did not pay, the dollar amount would go up immensely. For every day that went by, that interest would compound. Maybe by putting this pressure of late fees, then the defendant would feel the urgency to pay his debt. I did not think a lot about the effects of this compounding interest. Evidently, it put enough pressure on him because once springtime rolled around, I received a call from my attorney. He stated that he had in his office, right there in his hand, the money that we had agreed to settle out of court on. He informed me that I should be looking out for a federal expressman to come knocking at my door within the next week. He also added that "The compounded dollar amount will follow within the next thirty days."

Within three days, early in the morning, there was a knock at my door. Oh, the beauty of springtime. It brings forth. I greeted the man at the door with a smile because *I knew that; I knew* what was about to happen. Closure. New beginnings.

My daughter and I dolled ourselves up extra quickly that day and headed into town to the local bank to open a new account with what felt like newfound mafia money. In the past, when I would receive a bulk of money from selling houses, there was always a joy connected to it because I had earned it. This was different. I felt like this money needed to be used to *help the child within me rise up.*

Two... Four... Six... O My

I began thinking about what I could do to complete the healing in me that needed to be done in this area of my life. I pondered about it for about three months. I made some phone calls to the city to determine the rules in trying to decide if I could have horses on my property and what the rules and regulations were for the ten acres I lived on. The very casual lady on the phone informed me that they didn't really have any regulations on the books about how many acres vs. how many horses that I could have on my property or at least none that she cared to research. Determined to get a definitive answer, I called a few other different government departments asking the same questions, all to no avail. Finally, after a handful of calls, the last lady I reached informed me that all the calls I had made had gone to the same room in the same building and that they were all sitting right next to each other. The answers were not going to change. Embarrassed. Small town. This is not California anymore.

I ran the subject by my husband briefly, and he did not seem to care one way or the other.

Spontaneity had become my friend. I always enjoyed exploring new, different avenues in life.

Miniature horses. They were always so cute. Long tails that hit the ground. Their overly long untrimmed mains that covered their eyes. After all, I did have a hair license for the past twenty years at his point. *This could be healing*, I thought. This would make my inner child a happy camper. After all, didn't my old doctor tell me on our final farewell not to forget to nurture that inner child? Nurturing it was.

Weeks later, my daughter and I spotted a handmade sign on the side of the road for a local miniature horse breeder. We drove down the gravel road with the intention of buying two minis. When we showed up, they had hundreds of minis. Yes, hundreds. They had so many that they had an old house on their property that they had taken the doors off and the glass windows out off, and the horses were running through it like a playground. It was so odd and yet so thrilling at the same time. Like the feeling that a kid gets the first time that they go to Disneyland.

We were soon schooled that there were different qualities of horses. There were registered show horses, which they obviously favored. They were very pricey and had no imperfections and had already been trained for showing prancing around with fancy braids and bows in their hair.

There were the medium-level horses that had yet to be trained but that had all the perfected genetics. These were the horses that most average people gravitated toward.

Then they had what they called the "rejects." The lame, possibly the blind in one eye...the untrainable. Immediately, wouldn't you know what I was leaning toward? I saw their brokenness. I thought they could use being loved.

There was every color possible to pick, from tan, cream-colored, brown, white, silver, black, and some they called paint, which was a mixture of two colors. I had never seen anything quite so chaotic. Miniature horses were running and jumping everywhere like one big carnival.

I asked if I could see the mom that began all this chaos. They introduced me to Dolly and began to brag about all her awards that she had won in the different state fairs. Dolly was only to be purchased at an amount I was not willing to pay.

As much as they tried to steer me toward their idea of a perfect horse for me, out of the corner of my eye, I looked over into this one caged section, and there lay all the rejects.

My adventure to buy two horses quickly turned to four as I listened to this husband and wife in a complaining manner spitting out insult after insult concerning this *bunch of reject horses*. The more they insulted, the more I was drawn to rescuing them from this life they were doomed to. The better-quality horses were fed hay and grain while the rejects were given the slop of the last night's leftover. Truth.

Right away, once my brain was able to calculate what was going on, I told them that "I will take six of your rejects." Their faces visibly showed their shock. One by one, my daughter and I picked them out. I say pick them, but I mean pointed them out because they were so wild that you could not approach or touch them. This husband and wife cussed and fought as they tried their best to wrangle these wild horses as fast as they could before we changed our mind, shoving them in the way to the small horse trailer. I did all I could to bite my tongue and get these horses on their way to a better life. Mean people.

I called my husband during his busy workday to let him know, "Hey honey, I shrunk the horses... I have been shopping... I bought six of them."

"Six of what?" he asked.

"Six miniature horses. I'm bringing them home."

"Where are you going to put them?" he asked, "We don't even have a fence."

"Oh, no worries, we will build one..."

Busy weekend.

By this point, all three of my kids had moved to Kentucky. My boys and my husband spent some quality time slinging a hammer to get that fence up quickly. I had no idea that God had some very peculiar healing techniques that he intended to dole out to me by way of housing these horses.

All six horses came with papers stating that they were registered with the state of Kentucky. None of this was of importance to me. What was most important to me was the way that I felt for the first time in a long, long time.

I felt emotionally safe when I would go out and spend time with the horses. They had all come with names, and I liked their names. There was Sky, Rae, Royal, Dixie, Jewel, and Bay. Out of the six horses, four were somewhat tame, meaning we could touch them. Two, Dixie and Jewel, never did tame. They had major scarring on them where some trauma had occurred in their life. They would stay within an arm's distance from me. Distrust: a behavior that I understood all too well. I still fed them watermelons along with the other horses.

Unrealized by me, God was healing me in areas that I really had no clue about. It was not something that the Holy Spirit specifically said, "I am going to heal you here." He just started mending my heart. Stitching me up. Repairing the breach so that I would be able to walk in the path that He had once called me to walk in. Right standing with God.

Those grocery store folks got to know us Cali folks well. We would make weekly trips to the in-town grocery store and buy fifty pounds of carrots and possibly ten watermelons, along with any other juicy produce that caught my eye. The horses loved apples. Their preference was that red ripe watermelon, though.

Once I got to Kentucky, got settled in my house, and for the most part felt like I neatly filed away my past, there became a surety that was building within me. One that I thought I had lost but had never fully grasped because, after all, does not Jesus say that you must lose yourself to be found?

"For whosoever will save his life shall lose it: and whosoever will lose his life for my sake shall find it" (Matthew 16:25).

God assured me that He was going to do a new thing within my family and me. I have clung to that promise wholeheartedly, hoping and believing and, of course, trusting.

Back to Hair Dressing

Since I was out in the country, God was able to mend me back together enough that I was able to have ample confidence to start hairdressing again in the small town that we had moved to. God gave me a mother and daughter manager and co-manager team who had lived a very simple and godly life. They were trustworthy. I was able to work underneath them as an employee, something that I had found so uncomfortable to do in the past. Leave it up to God to give me two women bosses to replace the men bosses I had had in real estate for so long. God was slowly rebuilding me one brick at a time. I am friends with the daughter to this day. Artistic flare reignited once again.

"Beloved, I wish above all things that thou mayest prosper and be in health, even as thy soul prospereth" (3 John 1:2).

Though I was wounded, I was also a mature Christian. God began to show me that He wanted me whole. That He wanted me healthy. In health, He meant body, soul, and spirit to be one. No longer warring one against the other. God had to beckon me with His love into believing that I was worth it. That I was worth being in good health. That I was worth God prospering my soul. Even while all my material things were visibly dwindling, it was my soul that needed to be healthy. He wanted me to know my value.

Time to Slow Down

Living out in the country had brought me a newfound freedom that living in the city never did fulfill. It brought a relaxation about me that I had never experienced. It is a slower pace of life. Literally, everything moves slower. People walk slower. People talk slower. The gal at the register is in no big hurry to check you out. I internally began to relax and acclimate to the lifestyle in which I was now living in. It seemed like, for the first time in many years, I was learning what the word *relax* actually meant.

This was something that I had always envied about my husband. He was raised in the small town of Winslow, Arizona. The nickname for that time was The Slow. The only thing that went *fast* through that town was the train. With his help and the help of the Lord, I was learning to let the Kentucky breezes blow against my face. To slow down and just be. Beautiful fireflies.

I remember walking through bookstores and, on several occasions, seeing this one book that read *Life After Antidepressants*. I remember thinking, *Oh, that will never be me.*

After all, the last words that the doctor spoke to me were that "...because of the trauma that you have experienced in your life, you will probably always have to use medication to function." I remember thinking if there was ever going to come a time for me. Would my time be now? It was as if the Lord would say to me, "Not yet my child, but one day soon." So I hung onto that hope that possibly one day I too would be able to get off these antidepressants; because, after all, do not faith and hope go hand in hand? I had the faith, and I surely had hope. God would say to me, "One day soon." Little did I know *soon* would involve many years of soulful healing.

Go Forth

In my journaling and in parallel times of writing, God would speak to me to *go forth*. Not fully acknowledging that this phrase is in the Bible several times, I always interpreted "*go forth*" as meaning *proceed forth* with filing a civil case against the Pedi. Years later, I now understand that it had multiple facets of understanding to it. In addition to this, it also meant for me to *go forth* and to march on without looking back, and just recently, as of a couple of years ago, the term "*go forth*" meant writing this book. Is that not cool? God is a God of multiplication. He can take one meaning in the Bible and make it mean numerous things in your life. Love that multiplication equation.

God began to encourage me to discover what it was that I was good at and to do a lot of it. When we moved to Kentucky, we closed Lil Cindy's Cookie Castle, but we took our ovens with us. I had the pleasure of doing what I knew that I was good at. As the healing in me continued, baking remained very therapeutic. It was an area of my life that though I was not baking for anyone special, I could bake for the Lord and then find someone to eat it afterward. As God was untangling me from all those strings, I was becoming better equipped to know about His almightiness. I was beginning to understand the scripture that said the beginning of wisdom was to fear God (Proverbs 9:10). My sense of entitlement was quickly vanishing. Oh, how many times had the Lord untangled me and my feet from going into areas I was not invited into? How many times had God cautiously and graciously untangled the webs that I had woven myself into?

"I will bless the Lord at all times: his praise shall continually be in my mouth" (Psalm 34:1).

As I continued to *go forth* in obedience toward God, seeking God, knowing God, and loving God, my mind became clearer and more determined than ever to be a success in life. You see, I learned that success is not what you achieve, but it is *who you are*. God wanted me to be emotionally and spiritually available to help feed the body of Christ. The more *untangled I became* from the darkness that tried to befall me, the clearer my path in Christ became to me. He wanted me to *go forth* and help the body of Christ, in particular, victims of incest. Somehow the reward of money felt cheap. I looked for every possible way that God would have me use the financial gain that I had achieved through the civil lawsuit to do something God could and would honor. I helped all three of my children in one way or another as well as looked for areas in the body of Christ where there were needs. I paid back my mother as well as paid back all the copay money owed to my doctor.

God showed me that He was my reward, my shield, my provider, and my protector; to Him, I was to lean, and that He would go before me, and that I was his chosen child.

He cares about you. About what your life will be or will turn out to be. He rewards obedience. He double rewards first command obedience. One of the roles that a Pedi plays with his victim is a servant/master role-playing. All my life, I have had difficulties with taking orders from anyone. Most assuredly, after the molestations stopped. So to take orders from God, which is how sometimes I looked at it, became very difficult for me. Where the Pedi had ill will only intended for me, my God had only good. Where the Pedi wanted to harm me, my God wanted to prosper me. God does not look at what is difficult for you. God does not play on your strengths. He instead becomes your strength at your point of weakness. He rewards obedience. He assured me that soon, very soon, a.k.a. twenty years later, my pure reward from the almighty heart of God with sincerity of soul—yes, I believe God has a soul—was coming. I was to wait in a patient mode. A prayerful mode. That the *blesser of life* would see fit to *yield forth* my reward. Go forth it was.

And he shall bring forth thy righteousness as the light, and thy judgement as the noonday. Rest in the Lord, and wait patiently for him: fret not thyself because of him that prospereth in his way, because of the man who bringeth wicked devices to pass. Cease from anger, and forsake wrath: fret not thyself in any wise to do evil. For evildoers shall be cut off: but those that wait upon the Lord, they shall inherit the earth.

Psalm 37:6–9

If you continue reading through this Psalm, the remaining of the chapter very clearly states that we are to not look at the wealth of a person in determining how well that person is or is not doing. A righteous man, while he may have little, he actually has much. So, while I felt like I had so many ungathered and unorganized thoughts and emotions, and I did, what I had going for me was right standing with *the Father,* and that counts for eternity.

Learning to Ponder and Praise

Once this part of my life had ended, there was a new phase of my life that I was entering. It was a journey to complete healing and deliverance of my mind and soul. The violations done against my body were one thing, but the damage that they had been done to my mind was a whole other, if not worse, defilement.

I needed God more than ever to come into my existence and clean up my wounded mind. I lived a clean life. No drinking, no drugs, no smoking, etc., all but the antidepressants, which I needed to use at this time in my life. No more little white pills. I dotted all my *Is* and crossed all my *Ts*.

I even paid the registrations on my cars on time. All the aspects of my life appeared to be in order. Appeared. My problem was that I was still in pain from all these memories. I really did not know what to do with them all. It was uncharted territory for modern-day psychologists. Should I put them on a shelf? Should I take them down one by one as I can and deal with them? I wanted to just forget about it, but each day that I woke, they were fresh on my mind. I would ask God why he did...how could he...but God remained silent. No answer to be heard for miles. No echoes. No Holy Spirit giving me fresh revelation. Just a whole lot of emotional pain.

One second, I felt okay, decent, normal, and another second, I would feel dirty and vile, smelly and just wrong. Yet another second, I felt faith-filled and ready to take on any battle that came my way. It was a mess. I was a mess. I had to pick up and keep going forward and try my hardest to quit looking back. O grace, lovely grace.

God graciously had moved my family and me to the South. For the next twenty years, He would each day heal me. Day by day, He would introduce me to a new level of *grace and love* in one way or another. I would like to be able to say that speaking out to the public about what my Pedi had done made it all better, but it is quite the opposite. It instead opened my wound wide open, subject to exposure. I am fully convinced that exposure for me was necessary. A demand, if you will, of God. It was a wound that needed to be opened, dried out, scabbed over, and then healed. This takes time. I struggled with feelings like *why couldn't he just keep his filthy hands off me?* Why me? Hadn't I already suffered enough? With lifelong scarring, was I not already ugly enough? You see, being molested made me feel uglier than I already felt. I had a long road of emotional healing ahead of me.

I wondered why God had not protected me from all this Pedi's evil. Why did He allow my mom to marry him in the first place? So much pondering. So many questions. None really to this day that I have gotten any definitive answers to. I have, however, gotten this one very important response from the Lord: That I am one of God's sheep and that I am to *go forth* and help feed God's flock. That He is the *Good Shepherd* and the feeder of my soul. I am to have confidence in believing that He is going to make everything right. Eventually.

"And we know that all things work together for the good to them that love God, to them that are the called according to His purpose" (Romans 8:28).

It is not my job to tell God how to run the universe. It is my responsibility to obey His commands. I tried to *hold out* on God like I was going to blackmail Him with my feelings. That does not work with God either. He is not to be bullied or to be *put in a box.* I tried all the tactics that I had been taught to do in the flesh as a child, and none of them came to any avail. *God works in the spirit realm.* His thoughts are higher than ours.

"God is a Spirit: and they that worship Him must worship Him in spirit and in truth" (John 4:24).

All that I could do was to lay myself down at the feet of Jesus day after day and ask Him to humbly remove all my shortcomings and character defects and to heal me. Yes, character defects. Each time that I was molested or abused, it warped my true character into a very odd format. I needed God to come in and reshape and reform me into who He created me to be in the first place. Humility got me further than I could ever have imagined. It helped to bring me to a place of sorrow. A sorrow that I had to let go of eventually. I had sulked in it for far too long.

Once the time was up that God had allowed for me to live in it, He eventually said that *time was up,* and I was to *let the sorrow go* or, as some would interpret it, feeling sorry for myself. No more sorrow. No more mourning. The time for mourning was over. God wanted to give me beauty for ashes, the oil of joy for mourning, and the garment of praise for the spirit of heaviness. That I might be called the tree of righteousness as spoken of in Isaiah 61:3.

I finally had a slight glimpse of an answer. All this sin and filth was perpetuated onto me to do its best to try and keep me from praising God and making Him Lord of lords and King of kings. So I decided many years into recovery, yes, into my emotional *recovery,* that praising God in the midst of *it all* was going to get me further in life, in my everyday existence of a life, than sulking in the sorrow and complaining about what had been done to me. Make no mistake; this took years for me to get to. Years of persistently pressing in. Ultimately, I got there, and that is what counts. An overcomer I was in Jesus' name.

"For your shame ye shall have double; and for confusion they shall rejoice in their portion: therefore in their land they shall possess the double: everlasting joy shall be unto them" (Isaiah 61:7).

No more questioning God's silence; I instead decided to trust God's silence. All the time that I wasted pondering on those questions and whining and crying and complaining, I was good at it, about what could have been and what should have been, and instead, I poured my tears out to Christ and asked Him for help.

Some may ask why it took me so long to swim through all the pain. To this, I answer...we all swim at our own pace. I have never been a strong swimmer.

I was so angry for far too long. This pain was way worse than the burns ever were. I just did not get how a person could do this to me, an innocent child. I was living in it, and I could not get out of it. I tried begging God, and I pleaded with Him to please take this pain away. He would tell me that *you first must walk through it*. He would say to me, "Trust Me. Commit your ways to Me and give Me your hand, and I will walk you through it and praise Me while walking through the valley." The only thing that would lift it was *praise*. I think going through it all that He was trying to get me to a point of keeping my head held high with *integrity* and *acknowledging* that I had done nothing wrong to cause this to happen to me. The Pedi was the sick one, and he tried to take that sickness and project it off onto me. He kept trying to get me to join his sickness party.

I concluded that I just needed to walk in the belief that God could and would restore me to sanity. I would say going through this whole repressed memory thing just about took me over the edge, but I now have a heart for people who are going through and dealing with sexual abuse that I don't think I would have had before. I, in turn, spun it into praise.

Later in life, anytime these questions would creep into my mind, instead of pondering them yet again, I would turn my eyes toward God and worship Him. I praised God aloud, singing to God and singing about God. It is amazing what mountains get *moved or removed* while praising my wonderful Jesus. Oh, the wonders of growing in the Lord. I kind of keep it as my motto to this day. Any time the past comes to hunt me, kicks its ugly head up, and rears its ugly dragon face, I just say, "Hey Satan, I've already gone through this. God has released me from it, and you are not going to put me back into bondage to it. In Jesus' name." I have learned how to fight in the spirit world. I learned how the court systems operate. I have learned how to use the Scriptures to gain access to the throne of God. I was in the learning mode. I used the Scriptures to gain access to the mercy of God, the grace of God, and to allow that access to flow through my life. Out of this, I have become a better person. I do not know what I would have been, but I know who I am now. I began to *rise* out of the ashes and *recreate myself* in many ways. God is good, and His mercy is obtainable and free.

I had to recreate my career. I was a cosmetologist before, so I was able to use that as a backup plan and go into that field and allow God to use me to *speak forth, healing* to others that He would bring into my chair. Sometimes, I would wait until I got the actual hair color in their hair before I would speak an *uplifting word* to them. So they had to sit there until their hair had completely processed. You could tell they wanted to run, but they needed their hair finished. Locked them in with that tint bottle. I knew that they would probably never be coming back, but inevitably, about six weeks later, some of them would be sitting in my chair. Ready for yet another session.

Even in my brokenness, He was causing me to minister the gospel to those even more broken than me. It was in that obedience to minister that He brought me wholeness and had mercy on me. Sometimes you must strike while the iron is hot. In my imperfection, I was still obedient in listening to the *voice of God*. I allowed God to move within me even when I felt unworthy. God used that imperfection to help heal others and, in turn, healed me also. God's ways are sometimes so contrary to how the world works. Oh, the perfect heart of God.

I had to recreate and repair my marriage and the relationship between my husband and myself. It was in dire need of a B12 Holy Ghost shot. This horrible court case had caused such a gully, such a drift, such a deep hollow hole in our relationship. Even though we loved one another—we never stopped loving one another—there was still that horrible valley that existed. I believe now that my husband had to walk through that valley just as much as I did. I believe in the literal that two shall become one flesh, or in the scripture that says two are better than one (Mark 10:8). This was just something that we had to walk through together. We began to rise out of the ashes, and we began to claim victory and proclaim the glory to God in our lives. Hallelujah. I cannot imagine what I would have been if I had not gone through this and come up out of it. If I had stayed in the midst of the pain and dysfunction, imagine what I would have been. Giving the glory to God, knowing that all things work together for the glory of God for those who are called according to His purpose (Romans 8:28). I began to quote the scriptures that I knew by heart; I might not have known the exact book or verse that I had read them in, but the verses were on point.

Turn it into praise for the glory of God. That is what God liked. He liked when I had a good attitude. God likes it when we are confident in *who He is*. He wanted me to freely lay *my will down* at the altar because that is where actual freedom comes from, *laying your will before the will of the Father*. Submitting it over to Him. He wanted me to take all that darkness and spin it around. Let *it* be confused and tormented but *not me* any longer. I started speaking to the darkness, telling it to "Flee in Jesus' name." Telling *it* that I was God's possession and that he had no right in this territory any longer. That he had to flee. No more familiar ground here.

God liked it when I laughed. I learned to laugh. For the first time in my life, I could sit down and relax a little bit and enjoy a comedy, laughing at the satire. I began to learn to let my guard down with my husband and kids. I was *becoming real*.

I worked my way through the hating, the envy, the jealousy, the strife, and not to mention all the issues that I had with my mother. My mother had helped me with this lawsuit with regards to my memories to the best of her ability because she did not have much to give in her active alcoholism. She would answer questions that I had posed. God still required me to lay down all the pain of my past, and included in the past was the abuse I suffered at the hands of my mother. While I was being violated by the Pedi, I was also at the same time being verbally and emotionally abused by a mother. She was filled with hate and discontent with her own life and somehow found a way to blame it all on her children. I let it all go.

My burns were the turning point between what was my mom and dad's dysfunctional cat and mouse game that was going on between them. It was a two-edge sword relationship where they both had sick high and sick lows that they substituted for real love. My dad no longer came in as the knight in shining armor to rescue her. The fantasy was over. My burns sickly were the catalyst that marked this change. Whether it was subconsciously or not, she blamed me. I let that go also.

This abuse that I endured at the hands of my mother, both emotional and a little physical, was very damaging. I say a little physical because one thing that my burns did do for me is that they saved me from the more brutal physical attacks that my brother and sister Kathy endured. I remember many times being in my room and overhearing them on the receiving end of one of her rage-infused disciplines for oftentimes minor infractions. They were getting beaten for the stupidest things, the dumbest things, like leaving a door open and being told too many times on a Saturday morning (when she was too hungover from the night before of heaving partying) to close it. She would frequently take my baby brother in the other room to beat him. I would hear him screaming out to me, "Cindyyy! Please help me!" I could not help him. I knew better than to confront that woman, that dark force, when she was in a rage. I remember feeling guilty for the physical abuse that I could not stop it.

Now the emotional abuse I say was more toward me from my mother. She would say horrible things to me, calling me "conceited" and "stuck on myself." Just the wrong things that I needed to hear because I was already struggling from feeling ugly. It was as if she was taking the *heel* of her foot and stepping down upon my head, pushing it into me as deeply as she could. Just like she would smash the almighty cigarette out with the *heel* of her foot. It was as if she was trying to torment me emotionally. Emotional abuse that was unseen by others but was very visible to me. Abusively spat words that she would use as a weapon when she could inject them without getting caught. If she happened to get exposed, then she would always explain them away. When I ever dared to repeat these words, she so vehemently spat that she would go right into denial mode, pulling out the *she's crazy* card or calling me a little liar. The unseen abuse. She would just take her hand emotionally and just put it on the top of my head and smash me down verbally. She was going to put me in my place.

At the same time I was going through my sexual violations, I was also having to deal with the weight and depth and reality of the emotional abuse I suffered by my mom's own unloving hand. It was undoubtedly difficult, but I came out victorious. I had always curtailed the verbal abuse and chalked it up to having a young mother, but I myself was a young mother, and I never treated or belittled my children in such a fashion. So that lie of an excuse that I had made up for her all these years had lost its power. Oh, the unclouded truth that the gospel reveals.

Bye-Bye Lies

Lies can and will keep you bound. Lies perpetrated upon you are just as destructive, if not more powerful, to break than the grip that they have on your life. Once you come out of denial about the lies that have been placed upon you, then you must try your best to *deal* with removing each lie. It is not good enough to just remove the lie from you. In addition, you must replace it with truth. The truth of who you really are. When you are a victim of incest, the lie tells you that you are ugly; you are no good; you are unworthy, and nobody loves you. It can even go a little deeper with other accusations. Either way, you must unlock these false truths that have been oppressed on you, usually for years.

I began doing positive affirmations before they became the norm. I had little white index cards, and I would write down scriptures. I had them in my bathroom toothpaste drawer, end table by my bed, kitchen cabinet drawer, my car, and the side pocket of my real estate briefcase. Scripture is powerful. It never lets you down.

> *All scripture is given by inspiration of God, and is profitable for doctrine, for reproof, for correction, for instruction in righteousness: That the man of God may be perfect, thoroughly furnished unto all good works.*
>
> 2 Timothy 3:16–17

All the help that one would need to get set free from the lies that have been placed upon them can be found in the Word of God. I was never sure which index card I was going to pick up and quote to myself. A part of me picking up and reading these cards was a trust because I knew that I had written them, and so I knew as I picked them up and read them that I could trust what was written on them. When you are bound up in lies, your judgment gets skewed, but the Word of God never changes. One of the most damaging things that Satan can do is to try and destroy the trust between you and the Father. In reading these affirmations aloud to my soul, I was regaining ground that the devil had stolen from me and reestablishing unity with the Father through a friendship relationship that I now was beginning to understand. In any friendship that I had ever had, I always had a small piece of myself that I would hold back from others. I never quite fully trusted anyone, and now Jesus was requiring me, as is spoken of in His Word, to allow Him into my friendship circle, if you may. He wanted me to hold nothing back but to use a blind faith and to entrust Him with the innermost parts of my being.

For me to be fully set free, I had to begin to understand that, along with the lies perpetrated, came the shame, which we talked about earlier in this book. It is a combination of unlocking the lies and unlocking the shame at the same time. I had to find my buoy in the lost sea of destruction that had tried its best to destroy me. It was a journey that no one could do for me; however, God wanted me to trust those around me. Those who were encouraging me to hang on while God very carefully and cautiously removed the lies from my life. There were times when I wanted to just give up, but there was an even greater desire within me that wanted *all of me* back. Those who know me will tell you straight up that I will not put up with a liar. I have been known to call out a liar straight to their face. As my daughter puts it, "Momma don't play that game."

I hope that in the writing of this book, I have left a road map that an injured victim can use for their own path of healing. That I have given you enough information to help you in your unraveling process, to begin and finish your road to completeness. That through this reading, you will understand that you are not the liar but that the one causing the violation was the liar.

Ye are of your father the devil, and the lust of your father ye will do. He was a murderer from the beginning, and abode not in the truth, because there is no truth in him. When he speaketh a lie, he speaketh of his own: for he is a liar, and the father of it.

John 8:44

Understand this one thing, you were the victim, and they were the perpetrator. You did nothing to cause the offense. All the blame goes on the Pedi.

Freedom from the lies projected onto you should be your main goal when asking God to deliver you from the emotional pain of being violated. Freedom and liberty of the mind. A mind that can think and express itself clearly and not be suffocated with cloudy dark thoughts is available.

"Put away from thee a froward mouth, and perverse lips put far from thee" (Proverbs 4:24).

The Pedi projects perverse lies upon you, and it is your job to take those lies and get them from off of you and away from you so that you will no longer suffer from the perversion that they tried to place upon you and upon your mind.

"Avoid it, pass not by it, turn from it, and pass away" (Proverbs 4:15).

The Bible speaks clearly about the path of the wicked. You are not wicked. Your violator was the one who was evil. When the door of this violation opened, along with it, a door was opened and a path that allowed these perverse and wicked demons, father of lies, to torment you and whisper lies into your mind. You must take every effort and seek the deliverance of the Lord to be set free and to be bound up no longer in Jesus' name, permanently shutting this door so that your mind will no longer be involved in that *spider web of lies* that do not belong to you. I had to say, "Take it back, Satan. This is yours, and it is not mine...for I serve a living God who is pure, clean, holy, and undefiled." I had to ask God to give me back the purity in my mind and to restore unto me *the joy of my salvation.*

Hello, Truth

Though I was in a lot of emotional pain, God still expected and desired for me to worship Him. To go into reverse was ignorant. It was only going to land me in a trash heap of even more emotional pain. Stepping away was not an option. I had to go forward. I had to press through the pain and trust the faith God had given me and hang onto the only one who could see me through to victory to the end of it all. Backward was not an option offered to me from *God's menu plan*, so I chose the only option that was going to propel me forward. Painful it was, and painful it was going to be.

Easy roads are not always how it goes as a servant of the Lord. The road can be quite bumpy at times, but I learned a lesson through all of this: that *God is a Spirit* and that they that worship Him must worship Him in Spirit and in truth (John 4:4). I was telling the truth about what had been done to me for the first time, and I no longer had to live in the lies.

By *not* speaking up and speaking the truth of what the Pedi had done to me, it kept me bound up in a lie. His lie. His defilement of a lie. His illness. His sickness and his warped thinking. Well, no longer would I be bound by the darkness of his lies.

Through the process of being unraveled from his perpetuated lies, I was finding true freedom. A freedom that led to faith. A strong, unrelenting faith. A faith that drew me to the Father like never before. God is truth. Truth defeats lies. Satan is the father of lies. My lie was being uncovered. The lie of shame was being revealed. This shame had to flee once it was exposed as a lie. Behind all shame are lies.

Freedom was quickly becoming my friend. Jesus was my friend. He was the pure representation of freedom. You know in the Word how Jesus says you are His friend if you do whatsoever He commands and asks of you (John

15:14)? Well, Jesus was asking me to tell the truth. The truth of what had been done to me. Jesus was asking me to expose this person, this lie, and to *own it* no more. It was in the obeying of the revealing and exposing this lie that liberty in my soul was discovered. Your body becomes bound. Your body feels inhibited. You are physically constricted; at least, that is how it was for me. Some people may do the opposite. For me, I drew within myself and became inhibited.

Liberty to speak the truth and to not be bound by any untruths is where I needed to be walking. Boy, did I crave God's liberty. In learning to walk in God's liberty, ultimate freedom was released to me. Reaping God's freedom was a road none too familiar to me but was quickly becoming familiar each day as I took one step at a time toward acknowledging and accepting His promises. His promises to set me free and to no longer be in bondage to self and *self-inflicted lies* done to me by my Pedi. God had promised to release me from the bondage of sin and to help me by gently guiding me into a faith, one that I could believe that His Word was true. All His Word was absolutely true. All the liberty was mine. All the freedom was mine. I just had to claim it and believe it, and yes, of course, receive it. Yep...a little *prosperity doctrine* was going to do me some good. No longer were the lies going to have my mind bound. My mind was fast becoming free as God was granting me back the *freedom and liberty* that had been so methodically, systematically, and easily stolen from me. Lies no more. Bye-bye, lies, and hello, truth. Truth was becoming another one of my friends, and so was Jesus.

I had always looked at Jesus as a master and me as His slave. Looking to Him as a friend was not possible. The role with the Pedi was always that he was the ruler over me. He controlled me. He controlled my every step. Every movement. So for me to change my perspective on the role that Jesus played in my life, it felt awkward and uncomfortable, but it was necessary for me to change my perception of who Jesus was in my life. He was trying to come at me in the Spirit form as my friend and my confidant. Someone that I could trust. At this time in my life, the whole stature of my prayer life changed. It was not an exact day that everything changed, but within a few months' time, everything shifted from the way that I always thought that it was between the Lord and me. Where He was the illusive domineering master of a God, all of a sudden, I *could feel* that He wanted to sit down and listen to me. I would go out onto the deck of my new home in Kentucky, and I was no longer bound by the city living life. I could look out for miles and look at the fireflies and the bales of hay and the green, green grass, and it caused me to see God in a whole different light. That I was no longer a bondservant bound by the law, but I was *free*. I had read all about this in the Bible, yet I never quite understood what it was saying. Well, I got it now. Elated.

No More Skeleton Winters

We all have emotions, feelings, memories, some that we wear on our sleeves, others that we just tuck down neatly inside of our soul. God had started dealing with me on *no more skeleton winters*. He originally gave me that word for my sister Kathy for her restaurant, or at least that is what I thought at the time. Because she would have slow winters due to the harsh weather where she lives, He gave it as a *prophetic word* for me to speak to her. I remember writing it down the day that I spoke it to her. Not really like a good title for a book but just unique and different. Just like God is. I wrote it down and kept it in the back of my mind. I kept thinking that there had to be more to this *no more skeleton winters*.

God began to show me in the spirit how we, as people, including me, go through seasons in our mind of frozenness where we do not want to *feel*. When something is too painful to feel, people put it in the frozen mode. I thought, *Hmmm, interesting, God; I will get back to that at a later time.* God was showing me that He did not want me to have any more laziness by allowing the winters in my mind to take over. He did not want me to be like that anymore. He did not want me to go into that *frozen mode*. Similar to what a computer does, where it freezes up. He did not want me to go into that *pause mode*, that *time-out mode*.

Sometimes, say, for example, somebody offends you, say that it is a friend of yours, so you go into that winter season in that relationship. You just put them on pause; you just do not return their text messages. You just do not return their calls. I was used to and trained to shut people out. It was what my mother did, and I knew it all too well. As a child, I spoke about this in my first book, *Hollow Family Tree*; we would be placed in the corner for the least offense, for talking too loud, for not speaking up loud enough, or for talking back. Sometimes you could spend a few hours in that corner. You were not allowed to talk, move, fidget, or ask for a single solitary thing. What was a kid to do? You went to the winters in your mind. It took great discipline to stand in that corner. Particularly on days where you were told to stand straight and no more rounded shoulders, with your hands behind your back. You were not allowed to look to the left or look to the right. You had to look straight ahead into the corner. Where is a child's mind supposed to go? What do you think of for that whole time? All the role-playing went on in your mind. You would ask yourself, *How long is this one going to last?* I became comfortable hanging out in my mind. Not a good thing for a child. Lonely.

You just do not respond to them when they send you a card in the mail. There are times when it is not meant for you to respond. But what God was telling me was, "No more skeleton winters. No more shutting Me, *God,* out because you are in pain. In your life, no more being stuck in the ice cube of the winter and not responding." God has an antidote for the frozen mind. For a mind like mine that resolved to repress these horrible memories. The best description I can think of is if you are frozen in time, and then when it feels safe to you, you go, and you deal with, you get that frozenness to melt, to feel, to become a reality. From the very beginning of my salvation, not really realizing its significance in full, I would read the same scripture over and over. I felt that God was drawing me to it, *"For nothing is secret, that shall not be made manifest; neither anything hid, that shall not be known and come abroad"* (Luke 8:17).

That which was done in secret will be brought into the light. That which is done in the closet, God will bring it out of the closet. Never really realizing that He was speaking to me about this part of my life, the repressed memory, I would read the scripture.

310

For there is nothing covered, that shall not be revealed; neither hid, that shall not be known. Therefore whatsoever ye have spoken in darkness shall be heard in the light; and that which ye have spoken in the ear in closets shall be proclaimed upon the housetops.

Luke 12:2–3

Being made to stand in a corner felt very similar to being placed in a closet with the doors shut. When you were standing in that corner, my mother and/or stepfather, depending upon who was punishing you, would ignore you the entire time. The only time they would speak to you was if you disobeyed their commands, the ones I spoke of earlier.

Sometimes both my sister and I would be punished in separate corners but at the same time. This was a tactic the Pedi used. It was a way of separating us even further apart. If this was going on and being perpetrated upon me as a child, imagine what goes on in a Pedi's mind.

I do not quite get the whole fullness of the skeleton winters. I know that it has many facets and many different meanings. This is one of the strangest phrases in all of the years of my salvation that God has spoken to me. That was how I decided that it would make a very good book title because that is what I did, stay frozen in time, for all those years, with regards to being molested. God was going to have to grow me up. It was like I took a snapshot. Put it back, filed it within my brain, and thought, *Well, I will deal with this later.* I recently concluded that when I was raped by my stepbrother, it put this stamp like a lock to a safe in my mind. I didn't tell anybody; I didn't talk about it for years; it seemed like, in a very sick way, the grand finale to the sexual abuse chapter in my life. That would be about the last time that I could remember all the sexual abuse actively in my mind as I would analyze it years later.

In this same short blip of time, my mother decided to get divorced and remarried to her own marriage counselor, the dad to the boy who raped me. I was still in elementary school. Trauma compounded.

I became frozen in that area in my mind. Somewhere in the breaking point, my mind had to have thought, *I cannot take this. I do not have to live in this pain anymore; I will just shove it all the way back in my memory and never have to deal with it again.* I do not recall doing that; however, when I try to place a time in my life when I came to a decision to forget about it, this is my best effort. From the time that I forgot about it to the time that I remembered it in my thirties, there was never a time when I remembered being molested. It was like it just never happened.

Feeling trapped in the coldness of the winter of my mind, by the time seventh grade rolled around, I never thought about it ever again. But I did not forget the rape. I avoided and never spoke to my stepbrother, if possible, for the duration of my mom's third marriage. Five long years. I did, however, spit on his sandwich and served it to him one time. Revenge. I never dreamt about the molestations or never daydreamed about them; I had no snippets of them come across my mind. None of it. That was one strong mind that God gave me from birth. I recall my doctor had said that I had one of the strongest minds that he had ever met. He complimented me, saying that that is what saved me from insanity due to all the abuse. Powerful.

It was kind of like a frozen-in-time moment. It was not till I was thirty-six that the memories started surfacing again. For me, *no more skeleton winters* was God saying no more of putting your mind off for a later date to deal with. Deal with your emotions now. No more freezing your emotions. Saying, "I do not have to deal with this now, I will just—" and God is saying, "*No, Cindy.* We need to deal with them as soon as they come up. When they come up, this is what we need to deal with. No more just skipping by emotionally. No more emotional seasons of change, being up and down and all over the forest in the winters of your mind. But rather, you are to and will remain steadfast in the fall just as you do in the spring and in the summertime, and you will be just as content in the winter times of your mind. Your peace will no longer be robbed. All your emotions will be a constant balance. Even, fair, and balanced. Wholeness. No more ups and downs but a mature, levelheaded oneness of mind. A mind that leads you into a joyful, balanced chemistry of victory and peace. *No more skeleton winters.* No more, I say. No more, I command. No more times where your mind goes to a place where it cannot cope. No more emotional time-outs. No more reprieves from emotional life. But instead, keep both of your hands as well as your mind attached to My plow. For if you just have your hands on the plow, then you get to no avail. For it takes the mind to guide the plow. No more frozen in time places for you."

No more running into the darkness, a.k.a. winter. That is what you do, the opposite of what God would have you do. He wants you to run toward the Holy Spirit. No more hiding from your feelings. No more hiding the child within but allow the child to come and live through you. Because I was denied a childhood, the ability to laugh, giggle, be silly, God wanted me to learn to be a child again in my adult body. It was a part of me that really never matured until I let it out and allowed it to mature. When I repressed this memory and looked back and was able to analyze it, I also took the real child, the one who enjoyed playing and goofing off and having friends and keeping friends and *cut her off too.*

It was and is hard for me as an adult to keep friends. I take things to heart. I take things personally. The least offense was all it took. I had learned to shut people out to protect myself from being hurt. If someone offended me on purpose, I cut ties with them because I did not understand why someone would deliberately hurt me if they liked me or loved me.

Immediately, if I felt they were hurting me, it meant that they did not love me, so I would cut ties with them. By the second time and definitely by the third, I cut them out of my life. I quit communicating with them. That is what I have done in my past. That is like taking your emotions and putting them on freeze for your relationship. Pressing the pause button. Again, *no more skeleton winters.*

> *When thou saidst, seek ye my face; my heart said unto thee, Thy face, Lord, will I seek. Hide not thy face far from me; put not thy servant away in anger: thou hath been my help; leave me not, neither forsake me, O God of my salvation. When my father and mother forsake me, then the Lord will take me up.*
>
> Psalm 27:8–10

Even deeper into the *no more skeleton winters,* God was telling me that when I would go into this frozen state of mind, I also would freeze Him out. Like a vegetable state of mind. He does not want me to do that anymore. He is saying to me, "Hey, if you are walking through the winter times of your life and it does not feel good, I understand that, but you have My face to seek. Do not shut Me out anymore. It takes a strong person to go through the repressed memory." He obviously felt that I had what it took with Him by my side to walk through these memories.

The digging caused a complete family breakdown; in reality, that family breakdown and division were already there. I blamed myself for causing even more division in the family, but really, I was not to blame. I was the cause that opened the closet for extracting the skeletal bones out of the closet; in conjunction, God would speak to me, "No more dry bones." It was all beginning to make sense to me. What an amazing God we serve.

"To every thing there is a season, and a time to every purpose under the heaven: A time to be born, and a time to die; a time to plant, and a time to pluck up that which is planted" (Ecclesiastes 3:1–2).

In my life, there had been a lot of evil seeds planted. I will take it even deeper. There had been deliberate deposits of dark seedlings strategically planted in and around my life that were meant for deliberate harm, but God had a different plan. He wanted every last evil seed to be revealed, plucked up, and removed. He spoke very clearly to me this word, saying, "You were born for such a time as this," as spoken of in Esther 4.

God did not want me to walk away from the pain any longer. He instead wanted me to grow, thrive, and flourish, even while I was in the midst of the pain. Wow, what a high order of demand, but it was one that I was called to walk in and through. It was not as if God was forcing me to walk in the pain. He was commanding me to walk through the valley of the shadow of death and to fear no evil if I were to obtain what I was seeking...wholeness. I could have ignored Him; He would not have left me, but it would have been an area of my life that I never would have matured in.

"For God hath not given us the spirit of fear; but of power, and of love, and of a sound mind" (2 Timothy 1:7).

Early on in my salvation, at age twenty-two, this was one of the very first scriptures that I memorized. In what would become some of my OCD behaviors, I felt it necessary to memorize this scripture exactly as spoken of in the King James Version Bible. I actually made up a song, oh my poor children's ears. I would sing this scripture aloud almost daily for years. The part where it says "sound mind," I would sing, "Sound mind, sound mind, God hath given me a sound mind." I didn't really realize the first very important part to that scripture said that "...*God hath not given me a spirit of fear...*"; the part of my mind that was in the repressed memory state was locked up by fear. God wanted and did unlock the memories. He removed the fear and allowed my mind to burst forward in faith. Faith was given to me as a gift. It is something that I have walked in deeply, and I thank God for it.

He wanted me to walk toward the pain so that I could dissolve it and get rid of it instead of going to this pause, frozen, hurt part in my mind. God was saying *enough*. We may not always know how we feel, but God does. Jesus was used, abused, made fun of and taken for granted, talked behind His back, mocked, and ultimately, murdered. He knew how I felt. He was my number one encourager. He wanted *all* of me.

It is our responsibility to speak to God and keep the lines of communication open as one would do to a friend. When I would go to these frozen times with God, it was not a good thing. God was saying, "Do not do that anymore." A lot of people freeze God out. It is like they put Him on pause as they walk out the church door on Sunday, keeping Him there, making Him wait till they choose to *turn Him back on* the following week.

The word given to me, "no more skeleton winters," was also regarding my relationship with my sister. From the time of the molestations till current, our relationship has been put on ice, a.k.a. winter. Occasionally, we would progress into spring, summer, and fall. We would go through seasons of growth, and then we would inevitably hit a rock in the road. A dead end. This would put our relationship right back into that winter mode. You see, when the Pedi began to molest my sister and me, it stunted the honest growth between us from taking place. An evil root was planted, which caused a division between the two of us, and consequently, we were never able to develop our relationship in a healthy way. Instead, our relationship proceeded forth in a harmful way. A hurtful way. In a very sad way, we began insulting one another just as the Pedi had insulted us. We emotionally mimicked his character's defective ways. Our relationship, for the most part, remained in the winter months.

"Neither is there salvation in any other: for there is none other name under heaven given among men, whereby we must be saved" (Acts 4:12).

The Broken Child

The big question that weighs heavy on my heart is, what part of the abandoned look in a child's eyes is society's responsibility? What part do we ignore? How are we supposed to approach the situation with a fear-struck child? So many times, as a young victim of incest, I would try and give an adult *the look*. I would find an adult that I would somewhat entrust; in trusting, I mean I had been around them several times. They appeared nice, honest, and kind, all of which my mother was not. While I know that my gauge was off as a child, I would queue in on certain people and try and decide if they were worthy of my secret. Each time I just got to the point of quite possibly telling them my secret, they would betray me in their behavior. This betrayal would be confirming to my inner knower, which at this point in my life was completely off base, that they could not be trusted.

I had equated alcohol with mistrust. I would just get to the point of almost telling my secret to one of these now entrusted adult friends, and out would come the bottle of Coors. I instinctually would take several steps back and tell myself, *Not now. It is not safe. Just keep it to yourself.* And then I would reassure myself, *Whoa, I am so glad I did not tell them.* You know that *Don't Talk Rule* that is taught in all homes where active abuse is taking place?

A child of incest suffers trauma. In the trauma, their roots are exposed. What responsibility do we have as a society to reach out and help these stricken children? What are we to look for?

I can tell you that the first thing that I notice is zero eye contact. If you do get eye contact, there is usually a fear and loneliness in that child's eye if you can catch a slight glimpse. It is almost like when you are looking at them and you do get eye contact that they are in the bottom of a deep dark tunnel. They are like scared dogs. If you keep trying to look, you can catch them trying to steal a glance to assess you.

Be aware that a child of abuse has a heightened sense of awareness of all things that are surrounding them. It is something that is developed from being abused. That child is keenly aware when someone is trying to press in and get close to them. Be prepared for kickback. It is how they protect themselves. But do not give up hope. As that child, you are used to adults who just want the status quo. Who don't really care to get involved and interrupt their life. As that child, if you just put up a little defense, then you can watch as they lose quick interest. It is like an unhealthy soul tie dance. The child is looking for someone to confide in. In their brokenness, they are looking for a broken adult to confide in. Someone who can understand them.

You see, the Pedi teaches you not to trust adults. They teach you that all adults are just as broken as you. All, of course, except the Pedi. You are taught that the Pedi is the only one you can trust. They put themselves up on *the throne* as if they are *perfect*. Every other adult will let you down is what they teach you. *They* will harm you, and yet it is this stinkin' Pedi that is harming you. Twisted soul ties.

The second level to identifying a child of abuse is acts of aggression. Often, a child coming from the home of abuse has problems functioning in a school environment or in any type of social setting. They are quickly labeled *the problem child, the black sheep*, or *the scapegoat*. It can take a long time for that trust to develop and that child to feel safe enough to entrust an adult with *their secret*. Even then, when you think that you have created some sort of bond with the child, they quickly will back away one huge step at a time. They will distance themselves either by silencing or even in a disruptive fashion. It just depends on the personality type.

The question again that I am asking is, what is our responsibility in helping that child come to a point of trust? Do you just walk away? Do you befriend the parent to see if quite possibly that could be the source of entryway to be able to reach out and help that child? That is a whole new ball to unwind. Then you must deal with the parent, and who knows what that parent has gone through? So much of all of this is just overwhelming; shouldn't we all agree? Imagine how overwhelming it is for the child to be carrying around such vile expressions of hatred and mistrust to most all adult figures. Sad. Lonely. Betrayal.

The third level to identifying a child of abuse is obvious; it is when the child ends up in trouble. They get in trouble in school for one reason or another. They get in trouble in society by stealing in one fashion or another, lying, and even breaking the law in young adolescent ages. Small acts of rebellion against the authority that is not protecting them. While I do not think that it is our responsibility to save the whole world, I do, however, think that it is high time that the body of Christ steps up when these incidents cross their path. God may have placed them in your life for that very reason. It is a dilemma that, in my lifetime, I know most likely will not be resolved. I myself have not always passed this test when given the task to do so. I do believe, just as we want to win one soul at a time to Christ, we should try and go out of our comfort zone and *win one child to love at a time* or at least give it our best effort. Jesus did not live a selfish life. He was always on the lookout, always listening to the Holy Spirit and its still *small voice* guiding Him in what He should do in each situation. He was about the children. Shouldn't we be also?

"But Jesus said, Suffer little children, and forbid them not, to come unto me: for of such is the kingdom of heaven" (Matthew 19:14).

And Jesus called a little child unto Him and set him in the
midst of them. And said, Verily I say unto you, Except ye be
converted, and become as little children, ye shall not enter into
the kingdom of heaven. Whosoever therefore shall humble
themselves as this little child, the same is the greatest in the
kingdom of heaven. And whoso shall receive one such little
child in my name receiveth me. But whoso shall offend one
of these little ones which believe in me, it were better for him
that a millstone were hanged about his neck, and that he were
drowned in the depth of the sea.

Matthew 18:2–6

The final clue that you should be looking for and the hardest to see would be someone like myself. I hid. I stayed silent in the shame of abuse. These are some of the hardest victims to detect. As God began to set me free in my adult life, I began seeing clearer and clearer signs of abuse in children. It is something that God shows me in the spirit realm about that particular child, whoever it may be. I do many silent prayers. God will show me a specific situation, and through acts of obedience, I stop and say a prayer. In doing so, it brings me some sort of solace for that situation.

Eventually, these children become adults. In not dealing with the situation when they are children, we as a society inevitably, as does the victim, pay the price. They become lone adult lost people, living in their childhood pain, trying desperately to seek the face of God, feeling as if they will never achieve the long stride that it is going to take them to receive unity with God the Father, God the Son, and God the Holy Spirit. We either deal with it when they are kids, or we deal with it when they become adults, and God forbid parent another child out of this brokenness, and so the ungodly soul tie cycle continues. The devil laughs as we live out his lie, and he reaps his reward.

"Even so it is not the will of your Father which is in heaven, that one of these little ones should perish" (Matthew 18:14).

Faith, Hope, and Love

"And now abideth faith, hope, charity, these three; but the greatest of these is charity" (1 Corinthians 13:13).

The Bible very clearly states that we are to follow after love and not lies. Love cancels out lies. It is in the loving of a child that lies must vanish. Can we just go the extra mile and reach out and love each child with a smile? After all, God does. These children are the future generation. It is through the eyes of a child that often God sees fit to bring healing to us tangled-up adults. Sometimes we do not see *the great disconnect* in our own life until we are forced to see it through the eyes of a child. We see their innocence and how our own innocence was robbed at such a young age.

Do not turn a deaf ear or a blind eye away from the brokenness of a child. If you have had your blindfold removed and God has extended grace to you in your healing from your past to not be afraid any longer, then you too can help in situations that you may feel helpless about.

Always remember that your power to help others comes from the one true source...Jesus. As long as you stay connected to the vine, your branch can always extend to reach out past your comfort zone to help others. Learn to rely on the God of the seasons. Winter, spring, summer, and fall. He created it all. Find your healing and bring that healing forth to others. This is *the call* that I believe we are encouraged to walk in. Spring forth and help to pull someone out of their winter when God brings them along into your path. *Love is the antidote to abuse.*

Circle of Completion

Throughout the writings of this book, I have teared up and cried many times. This was not easy to write. At no time was it fun. But it was final. I have finally come to an end of an era of my life. When God told me to wait to write this book, I somehow speculated that He meant to wait a year or even five years. Never once thinking that He meant twenty-plus years. In the writing of this book, I underwent a healing project that I never knew needed to be gone through.

At one point, just a chapter into the writing of the book, my daughter, Deana Joy, said, "Momma, give me the laptop. I will do the typing." She could see how very difficult it was for me to lay down my pride and my pain and to just tell *my truth* that no one could take from me. I had to humble myself and take on the robe of kindness and submit to what God was telling me and calling me to do. Oh, the wonders of a daughter. So gracefully placed into my life. So unaware that God would use her in the helping of the telling of such a *tragedy* that occurred in my life.

For the tears, I am thankful. Without them, I could not have gained the higher ground by overcoming the pain of being sexually abused. I thank God for my daughter daily that she has a compassionate heart. A heart that understands a child. She understands the anointing of the Holy Spirit, as the first five years of her life, I literally laid hands on her and prayed over her *daily*. I can now see that there was a reason for it all. She is my bright morning star. The one who helped pick me up when I was at my deepest low. When my friends and family could not see the exact pain of what I was going through, she could see right through the mask, seeing it all. She is a better person because of the compassion that she embraced.

This generational curse is an evil weed with many roots. My daughter has had her own healing that she undertook in the writing of this book. I will even take it a step further in adding that she married and divorced two severely sexually dysfunctional and abusive men. Men who affected not only her but her children also. Because of this, she is able to write from a *position of authority* from the role of the mother in these situations.

Without her walking her own road of healing, this would not have been possible for her to even contribute to the writing of this book. She had her own pain she had to dive through but was willing to do so for the circle of healing to be completed. For her own children to have *a hope*. So for her to step up to the plate and offer to do the actual typing into the laptop put her into the position to confront many demons that were locked up in her own closets.

In the writing of the book, those generational strongholds and curses have been revealed and have lost their control, hold, and power. We are seeing victory in our next generation. Those strongholds and demons have had to flee in Jesus' name. She wanted her mother back, and she got her.

Speak Your Truth

I happened to be one of the fortunate ones who was able by the grace of God to see clearly that my time of reprieve was over.

Stopping antidepressants is not fun. Under the guise of the Holy Spirit, He ushered me back and spoke very clear and crisp words that it was time to quit. *The time was now.* God used the antidepressants to help me swim through a very tremulous time in my life. For that, I am extremely thankful and grateful. God granted me the desire of my heart. He clearly commanded me, saying, "The only way that you will stay off of these medications is that each time that you feel angry or frustrated, you be honest, deal with it, and speak your truth." I have never forgotten that. I lined it up with what I had once learned in a twelve-step program that anger turned inwards leads to depression.

Once I came off the antidepressants, there was a shift, which is saying it lightly, in our household. I felt like my mind was clearer than it had ever been in my entire life. *I see clearly now.* I felt a gratefulness toward God that I had never had before. I felt a connection with my nuclear family to such a depth, care, and concern. A depth that I had been seeking out my entire life had finally been achieved. I have a backbone about me that I have never had before. While I had always been outspoken, I now did not put up with any baloney. There are pros and cons to the use of antidepressants. I am not here to judge or tell you what you should do. There was definitely a time and season for their need in my life.

Emotionally Set Free

My quest for emotional peace was a journey like no other. For far too many years, I was emotionally tormented and physically bullied by my mother. I sincerely believe that the torment of my mind started about the same time that my mother began dabbling into witchcraft. As the practice increased, the torment increased. It was an entry point for Satan to have a stronghold in my family of origin and within my mom's life. Though to the best of my knowledge, my mom did not practice witchcraft to the depths that some would practice, she still willingly opened the door for Satan to enter by allowing it and introducing it into our home. My mom had placed her hands on the plow, got involved in a church, and attended regularly for a couple of years. She was accountable for herself and her minor children by openly defying and despising God when she left this church and to this day.

She had opened the door and given Satan access to try and devour whatever he wanted in my mother and her family of origin or offspring. Adding drugs and alcohol to the lifestyle that she had chosen only made it easier for Satan to attack her offspring. The struggles that I had to endure as a child of a parent who willfully denied Jesus Christ as her Lord and Savior were immensely torturing and tormenting. The sad part is that my mom was unknowledgeable of the real truth of dabbling into witchcraft.

Satan does not just go away on his own accord. He only increases in strength. There is only one way to remove Satan from your life and to receive the covering of the blood of the Lamb, and that is by calling on the *holy* name of Jesus Christ. One must be delivered of any evil spirits that are in their body or that have darkened one's spirit and soul. You must remove the dark and replace it with light.

My mom, to this day, leans on satanic power to handle or manage her life. God showed me to sever the ties in order to be free of the oppression. I chose to obey God's voice, and I separated my life from hers. I do still speak to my oldest sister, Kathy, on a regular basis. She is aware that I have separated my mom from my life, and she respects my decision. God showed me that in order for me to be completely set free from any unhealthy strongholds over my life, it was best that I separated, so I obeyed.

God was willing to protect me, but I needed to be willing to obey. God showed me that it was in the obedience of the separation that I had released her over to God. Now, God could begin to deal with her if she were ever to have a chance for salvation. By me holding on, I was only getting in God's way. It was in the release that I found a completed deliverance from any satanic hold that the devil had over me or upon my mind. Yes, it was that deep of a dark satanic hold. I had to release my mom over to God. Once I called it as it really was, all holds, all oppression, all curses, and all satanic prayers lost their strength. No longer did they affect me at all whatsoever. Amen!

You see, for years, I knew that there was a problem, but I did not have clarity about what the problem was. It was in my obedience to listening to God's direction that release ultimately came. All holds were broken. It was as if there were dark areas of unrevealed satanic demons still trying to control me in the background. I could feel *it,* but I couldn't see *it* in the spirit until, through the obedience of separating from my mom, Jesus shined His glorious light of the Holy Spirit in each and every crevice that Satan had tried to darken. Now, quite possibly, it will be easier for a person to understand that in addition to the alcoholism, there was the use of satanic practices in my childhood home. Her children basically became human sacrifices in this world for the devil's territory. Oh, the precious blood of the Lamb and the wonderful covering of the Holy Spirit.

Have I Done Enough?

Through the years, I have contemplated all that I had gone through, the police, the attorneys, and the evaluations, all of this. I had done all the proper steps. Yet still, there were not enough witnesses or enough evidence. This was really heart-wrenching to me. You are telling me that this guy can just do this to people, to little kids, and nobody can stop him? How is that possible? How can we not stop him? Even to this day, he is still out there. He has never served any prison time. Of all the people, I thought that I could be the one who could stop him. It just does not seem right.

While God has truly healed me and made me whole in the best possible way that I could be, I still feel bad for the other little girls who are now women that he quite possibly hurt. I do not know if God has set them free and made them whole. It breaks my heart because I know the pain that I felt until God came in and did His majestic, mighty handful of miraculous works on me. I feel bad for those girls who have not been able to experience any freedom. It makes me literally sick to my stomach. The fact that he had the power to take other little girls' purity from them is so wrong. I feel adamant that this needs to stop. I just do not know how to stop it. In writing this book, I am hoping that I can help stop more little girls from being molested. Just one would be a victory.

While you do not have your purity any longer, I believe that God fills you with His joy. I believe that because I lost my purity, God gave me an extra portion of joy.

"For your shame ye shall have double; and for confusion they shall rejoice in their portion: therefore in their land they shall possess double: everlasting joy shall be unto them" (Isaiah 61:7).

God will give you double for your trouble and then some. I hang onto that joy. I have a peace within my soul even though I am aware that as I look out the windowpanes of my soul, they are slightly tainted. With the heavenly washing and purifying of my soul, the long-stained windows of my soul are clarifying one pane at a time.

A contentment that reveals kindness. I carry that kindness and that joy inside of me, and I try to spread them around as often as I sense and feel the need to. As far as purity, that is never to be replaced, and that is a sad day for our society.

"Seeing it is a righteous thing with God to recompense tribulation to them that trouble you" (2 Thessalonians 1:6).

I had to give up on the tug of war. I had to believe that God was my vindicator. So I lay down during the battle and trusted God that He would repay them for their evil.

As for me, I will walk in the joy of the Lord as often as is humanly possible. I will hold my head up high in knowing that I did my part.

I walk in truth to the best of my ability spreading the *gospel of love* to the lost sheep of God's fold. And as spoken of in the book of Joshua, as for me and my house, we will serve the Lord.

Family Relationship Checkups

Often, when I read a book or watch a movie, I am often left wondering whatever happened to this or that person. I want to take the time to give you a grand finale checkup as to what did happen to each person, from my perspective, that played such pivotal roles during this critical stage of my life. I think it would be remised to not inform you of where everybody landed in this battlefield fraught with spiritual warfare that is my life story.

Cindy

First, I want to say I currently carry both a real estate license and a cosmetology license in the great state of Arizona, where I currently reside. In addition, I am an ordained minister of the gospel.

Most of all, I want to say that through it all, I was able to rise above the darkness that tried its best to consume me. Darkness works hardest to consume light. There has been a mighty calling on my life since childhood. All forces of darkness have tried their best to consume me and snuff out any light that existed, but ultimately, God prevailed. Love won. I am proud to say that through much travail, I am standing tall on solid ground. On good soil. Planting a good seed with my arms wide open to receive the harvest God has prepared for me to walk in. Who would have ever thought that I would have written two books and be working on my third? I continue from the great state of Arizona to try my best to feed the sheep of God that He has placed in my pathway. The pathway that God has planted me on. No matter what the day ahead has for me, my face is turned toward the Lord, ever listening to *His still small voice* in every situation, whether it be in the grocery store or at the gas pump. When God speaks, I am quick to hear, being not just a hearer of the word but a doer of the word. I remain married to the love of my life, Mr. Blue Eyes. I am honored to say that God found a way to repair that which was broken and make it whole again. Something only God in His infinite power can do.

My Devoted Husband

Stable. Balanced and consistent is how I would describe my husband. He enjoys his employment, still working in the electricity industry, but more than that, he enjoys having his life and his wife back. Something that he was not so sure would ever happen. He watched me go down for the count, and he also watched me, through the grace of the almighty God, wake up and yell to the world that it was my time to shine. To acknowledge that I was born for such a time as this.

As the years have gone by, I have had numerous conversations with him about this time in my life. In these conversations, he has acknowledged that I was born to be a mouthpiece for the Lord. That I was supposed to yell it out upon the rooftops. He acknowledges that he was supposed to be there to support me and that sometimes he failed badly on his part. I will always feel a sense of indebtedness for my husband for supporting me at a time when many other people walked away or distanced themselves, not wanting to be involved. There is a much more stable relationship between the two of us. Though we may have our ups and downs, we always have that Rock. You know that solid rock foundation, Jesus Christ, the healer and the lifter of our souls. True love found. Eyes of blue.

My Sister Kathy

Katherine's
Café
Amoré

Though Kathy was never able to get her life together for a long enough period of time to become a witness in the failing criminal case, she did try attempt after attempt of sobriety. I personally helped to enroll her in at least four different sober living programs. All were failed attempts to rescue her.

People do not change until they are ready to change. I had long already moved to Kentucky by then. My conversations through the years, for the most part, other than a few dysfunctional put-together family reunions, have been over the phone. As with myself, it took her far more years than she would have liked, but she eventually got off all of the hard drugs and moved to Arkansas. She was able to buy a restaurant and put her chef talents to work for her. She continues to reside there and is the owner of a successful Italian restaurant called Café Amore out of Eureka Springs, Arkansas. On occasion, she has been able to take a vacation and come and visit us. Her coconut pistachio creation of a pie is to die for.

Sometimes you must give up a relationship and give up your effort on that relationship to gain it. We have tried hard to put the past in the past and to gain new insight, higher levels, to a sisterhood that no Pedi can or will ever destroy again.

First, let me say that she is one of the most talented chefs I have ever known. Not to mention one of the most giving humans on the planet. She is a great communicator. Of course, I am a little biased; that is my sister. There is something to be said about living on the streets. When that person, God willing, finds the efforts and courage needed to try and pick up the pieces of their lost childhood, they become dynamic in a way that is unexplainable. You would just have to meet her one day to know what I am talking about. She is currently working on putting together her first cookbook. Cannot wait. Calzones away.

My Daughter, Deana Joy

Co-author to both this book and *Hollow Family Tree,* as well as a licensed Realtor in Arizona, my daughter has become a very strong, Spirit-filled, Spirit-in-tuned woman of God. While my life was just that...mine, she elected and felt compelled to re-walk through a lot of it with me. I believe for this reason that she has been given an extra dose of grace in all things that she touches in her life. She could have turned a blind eye when all of this first began to happen but instead had a heart for the hopeless. Being involved has always been at the heart of what drives her in her life. She is a peacemaker, *and yet she speaks truth using her two-edged sword to decipher good and evil.*

Having a divine call upon her life from birth, she understood that she was *purposed* to walk through this horrific time with me. She has concluded and reaffirmed several times to me in writing these two books that it is what she is *called to do* for the edifying and purifying of the body of Christ. It would not surprise me in the least if, one day soon, she starts some sort of an organization to help wounded sexual assault victims. This is where her heart lies. She is a helper, a helper to the fold.

Deana Joy walks in and understands the favor of God. She understands that all that she is and that all that she ever will be is due to the favor of God toward her. She understands that she is a child of the Lord, and she believes that any reward that she is to receive from the Lord is connected to the high calling of favor that she was born into. She is gifted as a discerner of spirits, exactly what is needed to call out this darkness and set the captives free.

While I'm saying all of this, there has also been a rough road for her to travel to arrive at this point. Along the way, she had two failed marriages, but through it, she found herself and her unique identity in Christ. She is mother to five really cool, smart, and spiritually knowledgeable kids. They are well informed in the ways of the Lord. She has made it her life's work to make sure her children know who God created them to be and to never allow anyone to try and replace that truth with their lie. Her relationship with each child is dynamic in its uniqueness. Her relationship with her children is anchored in the Trinity, the Father, the Son, and the Holy Spirit. She spends her days writing while her kids are in school, only cutting it short for carpool to start.

My Two Sons

Both of my sons married, and each had three children. They both found the Lord. My oldest lives in Kentucky with his wife and three children. My middle son moved to Washington State with his three children. They both have suffered but are working hard to walk upright. Striving to be good examples of what a healthy, nurturing father looks like.

My Lifelong Friend Joann

My lifelong friend Joann has always been just a phone call away. No matter what life brought us both, we choose to stick steadfastly together. She was a friend to me at a point in my life when I felt so destitute, scared, and alone.

At the beginning of our relationship, the Lord used me to breathe life into Joann spiritually through Scripture and rhythm and harmony and love. It became this beautifully seeded friendship that only God could have orchestrated. During the time of my memories being restored, Joann was there to bounce back all that I had fed into her in a way that was able to steady me. She reminds me that everything was ultimately going to be okay and that all things were in God's hands. That all things work together for good for those who love the Lord and are called according to His purpose (Romans 8:28). She is a true sounding board. She has become the extended family that I lost. She is closer than a sister. The dearest of friends. I am proud to announce that she, thirty-five years later, is still daily serving the Lord. I hope one day, when we both grow old, not too old, we get to live in closer proximity to one another. For now, I have accepted that God has us where He needs us, doing the work He has called us to do.

My Mommy Dearest

There is not much more that I can say regarding my relationship with my mother that I have not already spoken of in my first book, *Hollow Family Tree*. Let bygones be bygones and just go on.

My Declined Baby Sister Relations

While I know as a Christian that we are not to walk in fear, the only way that I know to explain this is that one of my biggest fears has come to pass.

My relationship with my baby sister had become quite pretentious. I am not going to act as if I know what it would be like, in any way, to walk in her shoes. As a child, I was the sister that she loved, who fed her babas and changed her diapers and rocked her to sleep in the middle of the night when she awoke to a mother who never appeared. I had very unhealthily attached to her as a surrogate mother. To go from this to find out in your mid-twenties that you had a Pedi for a father who had harmed this loving sister. One would think that in a rational thought, you would choose the sister and caregiver over the absentee father.

Sadly, as life would have it, people make their own choices. Sometimes those choices appear to be obscure. I have never understood her decision. This is a loss that I must accept. While she always expected me to respect her choices, and I did, the decision to keep the Pedi active in her life, that choice propelled me to make a choice of my own. Our choices are not made in bubbles. They have effects, and they sent us both down different paths. Paths leading away from one another.

Years later, she revealed to me a secret that she had kept from me. Some very valuable information was withheld that could have been an asset in the trial against her Pedi father. Information that would have quite possibly sent her father to prison.

One of the girls that was on my list, a close relative on her father's side, had confided in my sister that, in fact, this Pedi, her dad, had molested her also. He had paid her upwards of several thousand dollars for her to remain quiet and not say a peep while my case was ongoing, and yet sickly, my baby sister still had a relationship with him along with this well-kept secret. If I am not mistaken, that is bribery. To the best of my knowledge, that is against the law. Seriously, who was she protecting? It certainly was not me or any of his numerous victims. I had been betrayed, and that was not just a *feeling* any longer. Now it was a *fact*. Like I explained earlier, that is what Pedis do best: pit one victim against another. Yes, my sister was also a victim caught up in all this *mess* of a life. Manipulative magicians. As long as it stays in the dark, the Pedi can continue to stalk and juggle his prey. I learned this information in a platonic casual conversation between my sister and me. Just another day. She casually told me that this relative of hers wanted to extend an apology to me through her. This victim wanted me to know that she did not have what it took to stand up against this Pedi, that she needed the money, and could she please tell me how sorry she was?

I continued in a charade fashion this relationship with my sister for years to come, but the damage was profound. That relationship needed to and eventually did come to a final grand finale halt. Hurtful. I learned to just let things be and stop using my caretaking, forceful ways to try and procure a remedy, for God is the remedy and the repairer of all breaches. I do want the best for her. Role-playing no more. Minimal communication. Maybe one day God can and will repair this fragile broken relationship and make all things new.

Oh...how many times has the Lord untangled me and my feet from going in areas I was not invited to? How many times has He cautiously and graciously untangled the webs that I so foolishly have woven by myself? Oh, the grace of the almighty God of Abraham, Isaac, and Jacob.

The Pedi

Isn't it astounding how God works?

On June 21, 2019, the Pedi was murdered. He was shot and killed on a community-living golf course by a rival neighbor. Now, who is the victim? Bullying one too many times, I suppose! Point said. Much mercy needed.

Peace

At the end of the day, when all the night lights get shut off, is it not peace that we are looking for? Peace in our heart. Peace in our soul. A quiet and contrite spirit. My hope for anyone that is in need of what this book has to offer is that through it all, you can find peace.

"Open ye the gates, that the righteous nation which keepeth the truth may enter in. Thou wilt keep him in perfect peace, whose mind is stayed on thee: because he trusteth in thee" (Isaiah 26:2–3).

"Peace I leave with you, my peace I give unto you: not as the world giveth, give I unto you. Let not your heart be troubled, neither let it be afraid" (John 14:27).

So I say unto you, "Be afraid no longer." Turn your night light off. Trust God to be your *light* from here on forward. He is worthy of your trust. Remember to always walk in the gospel of love.

CPSIA information can be obtained
at www.ICGtesting.com
Printed in the USA
LVHW032241070622
720712LV00015B/348